TWAYNE'S WORLD AUTHORS SERIES
A Survey of the World's Literature

Sylvia E. Bowman, Indiana University

GENERAL EDITOR

CHINA

William R. Schultz, University of Arizona

EDITOR

Chiang Kuei

TWAS 320

Chiang Kuei and his bride, Yen Hsueh Mei (1929)

Chiang Kuei

By Timothy A. Ross

Arkansas State University

Twayne Publishers, Inc. :: New York

Library of Congress Cataloging in Publication Data

Ross, Timothy A
  Chiang Kuei.

  (Twayne's world authors series, TWAS 320)
  Bibliography: p. 155.
  1.   Chiang, Kuei.
PL2844.K8Z85   895.1'3'5   74-2172
ISBN 0-8057-2214-9

MANUFACTURED IN THE UNITED STATES OF AMERICA

Contents

	About the Author	6
	Preface	7
	Acknowledgments	11
	Chronology	13
1.	Chiang Kuei's Family and Youth	15
2.	Revolution and War	40
3.	Living and Writing in Taiwan	64
4.	*Breaking Free*	71
5.	*The Whirlwind*	76
6.	*The Two Suns*	102
7.	*Swallow Tower*	125
8.	The Lesser Novels and Miscellaneous Writings	133
9.	Conclusion	147
	Notes and References	151
	Selected Bibliography	155
	Index	157

About the Author

Timothy A. Ross is a native of Des Moines, Iowa. After high school and three years in the Marines, he attended the University of Iowa, Iowa City, and began his Chinese language study under Dr. Mei Yipao and Ramon L. Y. Woon. In 1961, he received his B. A. degree in Political Science and in Chinese and Oriental Studies and in 1963, the M. A. degree in History of the Far East under Dr. Chang Hsinpao. A grant enabled him to attend the Inter-University Center for Chinese Language Studies in Taipei in 1964-65. While in Taiwan, he met Chiang Kuei in Tainan and undertook to translate *The Whirlwind*. They have corresponded since then.

Since the fall of 1965, he has taught in the History Division at Arkansas State University, Jonesboro, where he is presently an Associate Professor. His Ph. D. in History of the Far East from the University of Iowa was awarded in 1972.

Preface

The high culture of Chinese civilization produced a long and illustrious literary tradition. In this tradition, the vehicle of serious literary expression was the *wen-yen,* or classical style of written Chinese, and the respected forms were histories, philosophical treatises, essays, and poems. Fiction was considered frivolous at best. Yet China did produce several remarkable novels, which have become part of world literature. The earlier novels, such as the *Shui-hu chuan* (translated by Pearl S. Buck as *All Men Are Brothers*) and the *San-kuo-chih-yen-i* (translated by R. H. Brewitt-Taylor as *Romance of the Three Kingdoms*), derived from the oral tradition. Through the tales of story-tellers, the incidents and characters of these novels became familiar even to the illiterate. Later novels, such as the *Chin-p'ing-mei* (translated as *Golden Lotus*) and *Hung-lou-meng (Dream of the Red Chamber)*, seem to have been the work of single authors. These novels were written, not in the classical, but in the *pai-hua* style which was closer to the everyday speech of the people and thus accessible to a larger reading audience.

By the early twentieth century, the classical style had grown so far away from the speech of the people as to be almost a dead language. In the second decade of the century, it was abandoned except for the most formal documents, and the colloquial took its place as the medium of serious writing.

This literary reform was only part of a larger cultural upheaval known as the New Culture Movement. Sparked by intellectuals who believed that China's moribund and decadent cultural tradition must be rejected so that the Chinese nation could survive in the modern world, the movement made its main appeal to the young. The youth were called upon to reject Confucianism and all kinds of conservatism, to discard such traditional ways as the custom of arranged marriages and the subordination of youth to age, and to seek actively both personal liberation and national redemption. These appeals called forth a strong response because China's situation in the early decades of the twentieth century was miserable indeed. During a century of increasing contact with the West, China had grown progressively weaker. The country was wracked with poverty, blinded by ignorance, afflicted with injustice, and disturbed by frequent civil wars and insurrections. To most Europeans, and to many Chinese, backwardness, venality, and fecklessness had come to seem ineradicably Chinese qualities.

In the nineteen-twenties and thirties, as China struggled through an agonizing period of cultural and political revolution, colloquial fiction came into its own and a great many novels and short stories were published. Most Chinese writers approached their task in the attitude taken by Lu Hsün (pen name of Chou Shu-jen, 1881–1936). This man, educated as a medical doctor, concluded that there was little point in curing Chinese bodies if their souls remained sick. He turned to literature and wrote a number of short stories, exposing the squalor and hypocrisy of traditional society. In what is usually considered his best effort, "The Diary of a Madman," the "madman" perceives the cannibalistic nature of traditional Chinese civilization. Although few Chinese writers attained Lu Hsün's restrained but sharply satirical style, most of them shared his concern for China's wretchedness.

This literature, characterized by realistic social observation, sympathy for the oppressed, and a generally satirical approach which put distance between the author and very painful subject matter, flourished in the nineteen-thirties. Further development was halted or diverted by the eight year War of Resistance Against Japan (1937–1945) and the four year Nationalist-Communist civil war (1946–1949) and foreclosed on the mainland by the Communist victory in 1949. Most of the noted authors of the nineteen-thirties remained on the mainland after 1949 but produced nothing to match their earlier work. Since 1949, writers on the mainland have produced a great deal of fiction but since it is written to political criteria, it has little literary appeal. In the Republic of China on Taiwan, writers enjoy greater artistic freedom but until recently the literature there has seemed insipid and immature.

Chiang Kuei, the subject of this study, is an outstanding exception to the above observation. Professor C. T. Hsia, in *A History of Modern Chinese Fiction 1917–1957*, singled out four writers of twentieth-century China—Eileen Chang, Ch'ien Chung-shu, Chang T'ien-i, and Shen Ts'ung-wen—who had "created worlds stamped with their distinctive personality and moral passion."[1] After reading Chiang Kuei's novel *The Whirlwind*, he included the author in their company.

The acclaim given Chiang Kuei by his Chinese critics was earned by his novel *The Whirlwind*, which dealt with the decay of a wealthy gentry family and the simultaneous rise of Communist strength in the author's native region of southeastern Shantung Province. Readers praised the author's fidelity to the customs and speech of the area and compared the novel to the *Shui-hu chuan* (because bandits figure largely in each novel) and to the *Dream of the Red Chamber* (because both novels concern family intrigues and the fall of a great house). Moreover, *The Whirlwind* was regarded as one of the few serious attempts to explain in fiction the rise and success of Chinese Communism and in fact this was the author's purpose in writing the novel.

Western readers will have to accept the word of Chinese readers concerning the accuracy of the author's portrayal of Chinese society and of course are not as immediately concerned with the question of Chinese Communism. Rather, for the Western reader the value of *The Whirlwind* and of Chiang Kuei's other novels should lie in their fascinating portrait of Chinese society during a time of violent transition. He has recreated in fiction the colorful social landscape of Republican China, peopled with an amazing variety of characters: scholars, bandits, prostitutes, wealthy members of the landed gentry, soothsayers, poets, revolutionaries, merchants, and warlords. Through his writing we are able to see Chinese society as it looked to a native, to listen in on a fictional argument between representatives of Confucian humanism and Communist revolution, and to perceive an overbearing Westerner through a Chinese perspective. Chiang Kuei is a particularly Chinese writer in that he knows no foreign language and has never traveled outside of China, although his Christianity and his anti-Communist political position do set him apart from most of the noted authors of his generation.

Since Chiang Kuei's novels are drawn largely from his own life and experience, I have devoted the first three chapters of this study to his life. Subsequent chapters deal with the four novels which the author regards as his serious work. The "pot-boilers" are treated in a single chapter, along with his other writings.

This study has been undertaken with certain limitations and certain advantages. The limitations arise from the recent political history of China and from the fact that since Chiang Kuei was not a well-known author until publication of *The Whirlwind* in 1959, little has been written about him by Chinese critics. Nearly all of my materials on the author were the author's own autobiographical writings. The advantages are those of personal association. I met Chiang Kuei in 1965 and have corresponded with him since then and he has been most generous in providing me with information on his life and work.

All translations from the author's work are my own.

TIMOTHY A. ROSS

Jonesboro, Arkansas

Acknowledgments

Grateful acknowledgment is given to Chiang Kuei for permission to quote from his writings and to Frederick Praeger Publishers to quote from the article "Literary Formosa" by Lucy Chen in *Formosa Today*.

Chronology

1908   November, birth of Wang I-chien, eldest child of Wang Ming-k'o, in Hsiang-chou Chen, Chu-ch'eng hsien, Shantung Province.

1912   February, paternal uncle Wang Ming-shao executed by imperial troops during suppression of republican revolutionary uprising in Chu-ch'eng.

1914   Commences Primary School education in Hsiang-chou Chen.

1916   Adopted by Jen Lan-yin of Kao-mi, childless widow of Wang Ming-shao.

1921   Commences Middle School education in Tsinan, provincial capital of Shantung. Obliged to attend meetings of Sixth Uncle Wang Hsiang-ch'ien's Society for the Study of Marxist Theory.

1924   Transfers to Chiao-ao Middle School in Tsinan. Joins revolutionary Kuomintang.

1926   Travels to Canton, joins Kuomintang Central Youth Bureau, takes part in Northern Expedition as Youth Bureau propagandist.

1927   Witnesses split between Kuomintang and Communist Party during summer of 1927, and repression of Communists. Flees to Kaifeng in Honan Province, then to Shanghai.

1928   Engagement to Yen Hsüeh-mei, a nurse. Goes to work in office of the Secretary of the Kuomintang's Central Party Affairs Committee as an editor of the *Central Party Affairs Monthly*.

1929   May, marriage to Yen Hsüeh-mei. First novel published.

1931   To Peking to attend Railroad Academy for four years.

1935   Employed in Railroad Office in Hsüchow.

1936   Writes *T'u-wei* (Breaking Free).

1937   Outbreak of Sino-Japanese War in July. Moves wife to Chungking, joins Chinese Army. Changes name to Wang Lin-tu.

1939   *Breaking Free* published. Undertakes seven-month walking tour, often in enemy-occupied territory, from Lao-ho-k'ou in Hupei Province to Nanking and back.

1940   Yen Hsüeh-mei joins husband in northern Hupei Province.

1941   Attends military-political training courses in Chungking.

1945   Leaves army at war's end, settles family in Shanghai, goes into banking business.

1948   December, emigrates with family to Taiwan, settles in Tainan. Business fails, bankrupted within the year.

1952   Completes *Hsüan-feng* (The Whirlwind).

1953   Wife stricken with paralysis, bedridden. Family converted to Roman Catholic faith. Finds work as caretaker of Catholic Church on outskirts of Tainan. Poverty.

1957   *The Whirlwind* privately printed as *Chin-t'ao-wu chuan* (The Tale of the Modern Leviathan). Adopts pen name "Chiang Kuei." Novel attracts critical acclaim.

1959   First commercial printing of *The Whirlwind*.

1960   Private publication of *Huai-hsiu-shu* (Sleeve Book), a collection of critical essays on *The Whirlwind*.

1961   May, publication of *Ch'ung-yang* (The Two Suns). August, death of Yen Hsüeh-mei. Chiang Kuei accused of culpability, tried, found guilty, sentenced, appeals.

1963   Publication in book form of novel *Ch'un-ch'eng* (Spring City) after serial publication in *Chung-yang jih-pao* (Central Daily News). Serial publication of long novel *Pi-hai ch'ing-t'ien yeh-yeh-hsin* (Green Sea, Blue Sky, Night, Night Heart or Swallow Tower) in *Chung-hua jih-pao* (China Daily News).

1964   Original verdict reversed on appeal, charges dismissed. Publication of *Swallow Tower* in book form.

1965   Moves from Tainan to Taipei.

1967   Circulates précis of projected trilogy of novels, collectively entitled *Ting-sheng ch'un-ch'iu* (Annals of a Prosperous Age), in an attempt to attract financial support. Publication of *Chu-men feng-yü* (Turmoil among the Prosperous).

1968   Publication of *Fen-ch'ing-chi* (Burnt Memory).

1971   "*T'ao-hua wan*" (Spring Freshets), a section of Volume One of the projected trilogy, published in *Chung-hua ch'ing-nien* (Chinese Youth Quarterly).

1972   Publication of *Hsi-yen* (The Wedding Feast).

CHAPTER 1

Chiang Kuei's Family and Youth

I The Wangs of Chu-ch'eng

SHANTUNG, a coastal province in northeastern China, has a long and proud history. It comprised, along with the provinces of Honan and Hopei, the area in which ancient Chinese civilization acquired its distinctive identity. China's foremost sage, Confucius, was a native of Shantung and so was his principal follower, Mencius. Mount T'ai, where China's emperors once ascended alone to perform sacrifices, lies in Shantung. Many of the incidents in the classical novels *Shui-hu chuan* and *Romance of the Three Kingdoms* take place in Shantung and in more recent times, the late nineteenth-century author Liu E set his novel *Lao Ts'an Yu-chi* (The Travels of Lao Ts'an) in that province.

As a coastal province, Shantung did not escape the attentions of aggressive Westerners and Japanese in modern times. The German Empire acquired a ninety-nine year lease on the Shantung port of Kiaochow and the neighboring city of Tsingtao in 1898 and the British leased the port of Wei-hai-wei in the same year. The Germans also gained by treaty the right to build a railroad line from Tsingtao to the provincial capital of Tsinan and to mine for coal along the right-of-way. With the coming of World War I, the Japanese, as co-belligerents on the Allied side, demanded that Germany surrender her holdings in Shantung. When the Germans ignored this demand, Japanese forces landed in Shantung and seized Germany's leased property. China, a neutral at the time, was powerless to prevent this undesired intervention.

Chu-ch'eng county lies between the port of Tsingtao and the provincial capital of Tsinan. Chu-ch'eng city, the county seat, was the home of the famed Northern Sung Dynasty poet Li Ch'ing-chao after her marriage, and in more recent times produced the noted

poet Tsang K'o-chia. In the early twentieth century, the area sur-
rounding Chu-ch'eng in southeastern Shantung was known for
three characteristics: many people knew German or Japanese, many
German and Japanese goods circulated, and many people had guns
in their homes.

Hsiang-chou, a walled town lying some thirteen miles to the
north of Chu-ch'eng city, was the seat of the prosperous landowning Wang clan. The Wangs of Hsiang-chou had reached the
height of their prosperity during the reigns of the T'ung-chih
(1862—1875) and Kuang-hsü(1875—1908) emperors of the Ch'ing
Dynasty, when they held over sixteen hundred acres of good land.
As members of the rural gentry, they lived off the income from their
land, which was worked by tenant farmers. At the same time, they
educated their sons to compete in the imperial civil service examinations. But as the imperial system itself declined in the
nineteenth century, the position of the Wang clan declined as well.
The last member of the Wang clan to hold an examination degree
belonged to the generation of Chiang Kuei's father and he attained
only the lowest degree. The clan's land also was dissipated and no
new enterprises were developed to replace it.

Chiang Kuei's great-grandfather, Wang Ju-ch'i, like several of
the wealthier family heads of the clan, selected a title for his dwelling place. Taking a line from an old poem, "Ch'un hsing tai ts'ao
t'ang" (Spring stars girdle grass hut), he styled his home Tai-hsing
t'ang (Girdle of Stars Hall). The Wangs followed an old custom of
including in the personal name of each child a character bearing
one of the five elements (water, wood, fire, earth, and metal)
recognized by ancient Chinese philosophy and each generation was
identified with one of the five elements. Wang Ju-ch'i's generation
was water.

Wang Ju-ch'i's third son, Wang Fang-tu, belonged to the generation of earth. In adulthood, he named his dwelling place Fu-hsing-
t'ang (Star of Wealth Hall). Wang Fang-tu was described by his
grandson as a "conqueror of wives" because he had three wives in
succession. His third and last wife was a Miss Ts'ai from the
neighboring county of Kao-mi. Although she bore him two sons, apparently he was dissatisfied with her and spent much of his time
away from Hsiang-chou on extended journeys. It was on one such
journey that he died, a few years before the 1911 Revolution, and

Miss Ts'ai survived him; she died at the age of sixty in 1918.

The two sons of Wang Fang-tu and Miss Ts'ai were named Wang Ming-shao (courtesy name, or *tzu:* Ch'i-hsüan) and Wang Ming-k'o (*tzu:* P'ei-hsüan); they belonged to the generation of fire. The family custom was to assign numerical rank, in order of birth, to all male cousins on the father's side of the family. The number assigned to those who died young remained vacant. Thus, although Wang Ming-shao and Wang Ming-k'o were the only sons of their parents, their family ranks were fifth and seventh, respectively.

Neither of the brothers followed a typical family course in adulthood. Wang Ming-shao attended the Industrial Training School in Kao-mi city and married Jen Lan-yin of Kao-mi. In the spring of 1911, he joined the revolutionary secret society, the T'ung Meng Hui, which sought the overthrow of the reigning Ch'ing Dynasty.

Wang Ming-k'o, for his part, seems to have adopted a deliberately eccentric and old-fashioned style of life which caused his contemporaries to look askance at him. Yet he possessed the strength and determination to educate himself in the practice of traditional Chinese medicine and to resist his mother's efforts to keep him close to home after his elder brother's death. When his mother died and he inherited his share of the family land, he soon sold it all and established a medicine shop and an inn in Hsiang-chou. In addition to managing these enterprises, he practiced as a doctor of traditional medicine, specializing in eye ailments. Thus, although landless, he became fairly prosperous.

Wang Ming-k'o married a woman of the Yüan family, well-to-do farmers in nearby Shih-chia-pu in the western district of Chu-ch'eng county. She bore him three sons: I-chien, Ai-chien, Ning-chien, and one daughter, called Yüan. The eldest boy, Wang I-chien, is the subject of this study. He changed his personal name to Lin-tu when he joined the army in 1937 and adopted the pen name of Chiang Kuei after his emigration to Taiwan. For the sake of simplicity, he is referred to as Chiang Kuei throughout this study.

Chiang Kuei's childhood, among the households of a traditional extended family, must have been a pleasant and interesting one. The family dwelling stood at a crossroads in Hsiang-chou and was called "Shan-hai-kuan" in honor of an otherwise forgotten official of the past who had once been stationed at the post of Shan-hai-kuan on the frontier between China and Manchuria. Shan-hai-kuan was not considered one of the wealthier households of the Wang clan. The wealthy households occupied dwellings with titles such as Tender Fragrance Pavilion and Bamboo and Pine Hall; they maintained two-horse carriages, kept crowds of male and female servants, and lived in a grand manner. But since Chiang Kuei was not allowed to go to these houses to play, he saw little of them.

II   *The Martyr's Heir*

The most important event in Chiang Kuei's youth was the death of his fifth uncle, Wang Ming-shao, in the revolutionary uprising at Chu-ch'eng city in February 1912. This led to his adoption by his widowed aunt and to his own eventual participation in the revolution. It is also reflected in his novels.

Dr. Sun Yat-sen founded the T'ung Meng Hui, a revolutionary secret society dedicated to the overthrow of the Ch'ing Dynasty and the establishment of a republic, in Tokyo in 1905. Most of the revolutionary uprisings sponsored by the T'ung Meng Hui took place in south China but the party was also active in Shantung, where members founded schools and established newspapers. A revolutionary atmosphere was created and many young men were drawn into the party. As mentioned earlier, Wang Ming-shao had joined the T'ung Meng Hui in the spring of 1911.

A revolutionary uprising in the Wuhan cities, located in central China on the Yangtze River, on October 10, 1911, signaled the beginning of the end of the Ch'ing Dynasty. The revolutionaries seized control of the Wuhan cities (Hankow, Hanyang, and Wuchang), and province after province in south, central, and western China aligned with the revolutionary cause by declaring their independence of the Ch'ing government in Peking.

The gentry of Shantung were already agitated by rumors of an impending German loan, for which the entire territory of Shantung would serve as collateral. Shortly after learning of the uprising in the south, members of the Provincial Assembly of Shantung forced the Provincial Governor, Sun Pao-ch'i, to transmit a list of eight demands to the imperial government. These demands, if granted, would have rendered the province virtually autonomous. The court's reply was conciliatory but the revolutionaries were not to be placated and they compelled the reluctant Sun Pao-ch'i to declare the independence of Shantung on November 15, 1911.

The Ch'ing court, panicked by the victories of the revolutionaries, turned to the experienced soldier and statesman Yuan Shih-k'ai. Yuan came out of retirement on his own terms, assumed the office of Premier, and dispatched the First Division of the Peiyang (Northern) Army against the revolutionaries. When the First Division recaptured Hanyang from the revolutionaries on November 27, Governor Sun Pao-ch'i lost little time in shrugging off his uncomfortable burden. He revoked the independence of Shantung on November 29, 1911.

After the revocation of independence, the revolutionaries in Shantung fared badly. The officials of the old regime were still in place and shortly Sun Pao-ch'i was replaced as governor by Hu Chien-shu. Under the rule of Governor Hu, the revolutionaries became hunted men and even those who were members of the Provincial Assembly were not immune from humiliating abuse. Meanwhile, disorders multiplied in the countryside and the provincial authorities found it impossible to cope promptly with a multitude of local uprisings and bandit raids.

It was in these confused circumstances, when the issue between the provincial government in Tsinan and the revolutionaries scattered through the province must still have seemed in doubt, that the uprising in Chu-ch'eng took place.

Chu-ch'eng city was attacked by the remnants of a band of revolutionaries which had failed in an attempt to occupy another town. After deciding to attack Chu-ch'eng, they secured the cooperation of a local bravo named Wang Kung-shuang, who lived to the north of the city and commanded eight hundred men. The attack was launched at dawn on February 8, 1912. The city was captured without difficulty, for the local students had been in sympathy with the revolutionary movement for a long time and they opened the city gates.

The local official responsible for Chu-ch'eng was one Wu Hsün-ch'eng. When the revolutionaries approached the city, Wu took refuge in the local Catholic church. While the revolutionaries organized a branch of the Shantung Military Government in Chu-ch'eng and established a People's Government and a Student Army, Wu Hsün-ch'eng bided his time. The revolutionaries, who were short of arms, sent a man to Tsingtao to buy weapons. During his absence, Wu Hsün-ch'eng, with the aid of the local Catholic priest, a German, was able to send a telegram to the government garrison at I-chou (Lin-i) informing them of the local situation and asking them to send troops.

When Wang Ming-shao heard that the Provincial Assembly had forced Governor Sun Pao-ch'i to proclaim Shantung independent, he cut off his queue, a symbolic act rejecting allegiance to the Ch'ing Dynasty. He wished to go at once to Tsinan but his mother's opposition held him at home. However, he organized a secret group called the *I-yung chün* (Righteous and Courageous Army) among his classmates at the I-chung Agricultural and Forestry School in Chu-ch'eng city.

When the revolutionaries seized Chu-ch'eng city, Wang Ming-shao's student "army" came under the control of a larger military unit but he retained command of it. He was assigned to manage the northern district. At the time, Chinese New Year was near, a time of celebration when all absent family members were expected to assemble at the family home. Wang Ming-shao had returned to Hsiang-chou and was prepared to pass the New Year's holidays with his mother, wife, and brother, when Ch'ing troops were rumored to be approaching. He assured his family that the situation did not demand his presence in Chu-ch'eng city but this was only to allay their fears. In fact, Wang Ming-shao knew that the revolutionaries had not yet gotten the situation in hand and he feared the effect of such ominous rumors. As soon as he could do so, he stole away from his family and made his way back to Chu-ch'eng city.

Wang Ming-shao arrived at Chu-ch'eng city just as the gates were about to be closed; only a space wide enough for a man to slip by remained open. As he was about to enter, he met a man from Hsiang-chou coming out. This man recognized him and tried to seize his coat to prevent him from entering. But Wang Ming-shao tore away and entered the city and the gates closed behind him. The man from Hsiang-chou returned there and told Wang Ming-shao's family that the young man was inside the besieged city.

The Ch'ing troops dispatched from I-chou reached the walls of Chu-ch'eng city at twilight on February 11, 1912. After hard fighting, the city fell to the Ch'ing troops on February 12. Then the slaughter of the revolutionaries began. Wang Ming-shao was captured, his hands were bound behind his back with wire, and he was whipped along to be executed at a spot outside the east gate of the city.

In the aftermath of the revolutionary uprising at Canton in April 1911, some seventy-two revolutionaries were executed by the government authorities at a place called Huang-hua-kang (Yellow Flower Hill) outside Canton. They gained posthumous fame as martyrs of the republican revolution and a monument was erected to their memory. When Chu-ch'eng city was taken by the Ch'ing troops, some three hundred revolutionaries were executed within the space of five days, but the event was little remarked. Their corpses were dumped outside the north and east gates of the city but no monuments were erected to commemorate their sacrifice and the place where they fell was plowed as ordinary farmland.

Ironically, the last Ch'ing Dynasty emperor's edict of abdication was issued on February 12, 1912, as the Ch'ing troops were fighting their way into Chu-ch'eng city. Perhaps the telegraphed message bearing word of the dynasty's end did not reach the competent government officers in Shantung in time to halt the massacre at Chu-ch'eng or perhaps it was simply ignored in order that some troublesome rebels could be destroyed.

Wang Ming-shao's unexpected and untimely death at the age of twenty-five (twenty-six *sui* by Chinese reckoning of age) left his young wife, Miss Jen Lan-yin of Kao-mi, a childless widow. Her first and only pregnancy, a few years after her marriage, had ended in a miscarriage. However, it was incumbent upon her to provide a son to continue the line of Wang Ming-shao. In the normal course of events, she would have adopted the son of her late husband's half-brother, a youth named Wang Chih-chien. Custom decreed this choice but Miss Jen disliked Wang Chih-chien, because he was the son of a half-brother and not a natural brother of her husband and because of the youth's cold manner toward people. After announcing that she did not wish to adopt Wang Chih-chien, she deferred the question of adoption for several years. At last Miss Jen made up her mind to adopt Chiang Kuei, the eldest son of her late husband's younger brother. For several years, Miss Jen courted the boy's favor by calling frequently at his home and leaving him treats

and gifts of new clothes. One day in 1916, at the time of *Ch'ing-
ming* (Clear and bright), a period in the spring when the Chinese
pay their respects at the graves of their dead, Miss Jen took the
eight-year-old Chiang Kuei to the mound called White Jade Mountain north of the city where the corpses of most of the martyrs had
been buried. Not long after this symbolic gesture of adoption, Miss
Jen announced her decision to adopt Chiang Kuei. Although this
choice was contrary to precedent, Miss Jen was not a person to be
lightly crossed; moreover, she was the widow of a revolutionary
martyr. Wang Ming-k'o, Chiang Kuei's father, also favored the
adoption and none of the ordinary clan members raised any objec-
tion. The only obstacle arose from the senior members of the clan.
Wang Yün-p'u, the master of *Chi-hsing t'ang* (Lucky Star Hall),
was the sole surviving son of Wang Ju-ch'i and belonged to the
generation of Chiang Kuei's grandfather. He was in charge of the
clan's register of adoptions and although he expressed no overt opposition to the adoption, he refused to register it. Apparently
Chiang Kuei's paternal grandmother, Miss Ts'ai of Kao-mi, was
against the adoption. In any case, after her death, Wang Yun-p'u
registered the adoption. Probably his decision was somewhat influenced by the gift of opium which Miss Jen presented to him.

After the adoption was registered, Chiang Kuei became a member
of Miss Jen's household in Chu-ch'eng city. After the death of Miss
Ts'ai, her mother-in-law, Miss Jen had become mistress of the
household in her own right. This household included, in addition to
Miss Jen and Chiang Kuei, Miss Jen's old maidservant, Chang Ma,
and Chang Ma's grown son, Chang Chiu-sheng.

Miss Jen came from a distinguished family; she was the niece of a
man who had obtained the *chin-shih*, or metropolitan degree, the
highest degree of the old examination system, in a special examination in 1903. Her husband's family, the Wangs of Hsiang-chou,
although declining, were still wealthy enough that family members
could count upon having their needs satisfied without working. In
The Whirlwind, which is a thinly disguised portrait of the world of
his youth, Chiang Kuei described the emptiness and boredom of the
women of this class. Women of Miss Jen's status, particularly if they
were unfortunate enough to be widows or spinsters, faced lifetimes
of leisure which they filled as best they might with friendships,
games, and opium. Miss Jen tried all of these remedies.

Much of her time was spent at the Mah-Jongg table. Her particular gaming companion was a spinster of Lucky Star Hall, of the sort who "ate their fill and had nothing to do." She also saw much of her two intimate friends, both of whom belonged to the wealthy household of *Tui-sung t'ang* (Twin Pines Hall). Miss Hui, a widow with a grown son, was addicted to opium, and although Miss Jen at that time did not smoke the drug, she would prepare the opium for her friend and keep her company as she smoked. Her other close friend was Miss T'ang, the daughter of a family of government officials, who had married into a distant branch of the Wang family. These women spent much time in one another's company, playing Mah-Jongg, or simply visiting.

Miss Jen's adoption of a male child to carry on the line of her late husband was in keeping with tradition but another consideration was involved. In China, which until recently lacked any system of public care for the aged and infirm, a compelling reason to have children was that they would look after one in one's old age. Had Chinese society not been torn by violent change, Miss Jen could have expected that in the normal course of events Chiang Kuei would have remained in her home, married, and produced grandchildren. Then, in her old age, she would have occupied a secure and respected position. Indeed, many of Chiang Kuei's cousins in the Wang clan did follow that course until time ran out on their way of life.

As it turned out, Chiang Kuei did not spend more than a few years in Miss Jen's home in Chu-ch'eng. He did not join her household until around 1918 and he left it for good in the summer of 1921.

Chiang Kuei completed the six years of Primary School in Hsiang-chou and Chu-ch'eng by the spring of 1920. He wished to continue his education at the Middle School in Tsinan. Miss Jen did not want him to leave but she realized that if she tried to keep him at home, others in his family would probably object. She let him go, and her adopted son slipped away.

After Chiang Kuei left to attend Middle School in Tsinan, he was seldom home. At about the same time, the old servant Chang Ma left Miss Jen's employment and returned to her native place to arrange for her son's marriage. Miss Jen brought another old family servant, Hsiao Wang Ma, to stay with her. Hsiao Wang Ma's husband had gone to Manchuria years before to find work and had never returned; she had no children. Before long, Hsiao Wang Ma adopted a young man as her son for much the same reasons that had led Miss Jen to adopt Chiang Kuei. This young man was Wang Chang-lin; he was married and worked as a mason's assistant. He proved to be a splendidly filial son and Hsiao Wang Ma was very gratified. In effect, Wang Chang-lin benefited because he was a poor man and his adoptive mother, although a servant, was comparatively well off. Hsiao Wang Ma received the warmth and affection which she might have received from a natural son.

Miss Jen came to feel that Hsiao Wang Ma had chosen better than she herself. Eventually she adopted Wang Chang-lin as her son as well so that she might receive the same comfort.

When Chiang Kuei, who by that time was leading an unsettled and wandering existence in south China, learned that his adoptive mother had taken another adoptive son in his place, he felt a certain relief. He knew that he had disappointed Miss Jen's expectations and he felt that he had also failed the memory of his fifth uncle, the martyred revolutionary. The knowledge that in her old age, and loneliness, Miss Jen had taken to smoking opium must have sharpened his sense of guilt. Thus, when he learned that Wang Chang-lin had taken his place, he was not resentful, but grateful, and he wrote to the other expressing his gratitude.

III *Chiang Kuei's Education*

Chiang Kuei received a rich and varied education which prepared him well for his later career as a writer. At the age of six, in 1914, his education began with six years of Primary School. In addition to the regular curriculum, which consisted mainly of calligraphic exercises with the Chinese brush and ink and the memorization and recitation of the classics, the students were given instruction in both ancient and modern literature after regular school hours. Their instructor in ancient literature conducted the students through selections from such works as the *Lun-yü* (Confucian Analects), the *Tso Chuan* (an ancient historical commentary), the *Chan-kuo-tse* (a collection of anecdotes from the Warring States Period, 403–221 B.C.), and the *Ku-shih-yüan* (Source of Ancient Poetry). From such works as these, he acquired the economy of style and the fund of classical allusions which appear from time to time in his writing.

Not all of Chiang Kuei's education was formal. His association with a comparatively distant relative of an older generation, his "Third Great-uncle" Wang Heng-Hsüan of Twin Pines Hall, provided him with an early and unusual introduction to the world of fiction. Ordinarily Chiang Kuei would not have been permitted to associate with an elder, but Wang Heng-hsüan, unlike most of the elders of the titled halls, was a jovial individual who enjoyed the company of children and allowed them to visit his studio to play. Wang Heng-hsüan was an artist; his landscapes were well known locally and were sought after, but he preferred to draw fanciful pictures of weird spirits in battle. The children enjoyed hunting through his studio for these pictures, which he would toss carelessly aside after completing. When sufficiently coaxed, Wang Heng-hsüan would visit the Primary School on Friday afternoons to give the students instruction in painting, but in fact he offered little instruction and much joking and talking.

Wang Heng-hsüan was an opium addict and the income which he received from his land went to buy the drug or to purchase collector's editions of rare erotic novels. One day when Chiang Kuei was in Wang Heng-hsüan's studio, Wang Heng-hsüan's brother came upon the youth examining one of the forbidden erotic novels. "You shouldn't look at such books. Come with me, I'll show you some others." Wang Heng-hsüan's brother led Chiang Kuei into his own library. This brother was even more of a fanatical book collector than Wang Heng-hsüan. He had been known to pay out five hundred strings of cash—the price of one-third acre of good land—for a single copy of the *Golden Lotus*. People in the countryside found it difficult to understand such an extravagant deed and in fact this man's passion for collecting fiction led eventually to the ruin of his family and his livelihood.

In the library of Wang Heng-hsüan's brother, Chiang Kuei discovered a fascinating new world of fiction. It was probably in this library that he first read the *Golden Lotus* and the *Dream of the Red Chamber*. Ordinarily, a Primary School student would not have been allowed by his elders to read these books because while both are acclaimed as literature, the *Golden Lotus* in particular is highly charged with eroticism.

The second stage of Chiang Kuei's formal education began in 1921 when he traveled from Hsiang-chou to Kao-mi city in an uncomfortable two-mule cart with iron-bound wheels. A simpler cart would have offered a more comfortable ride but his family felt that their status as rural gentry demanded a two-mule cart. From Kao-mi, a station on the Kiaochow-Tsinan railroad line, Chiang Kuei rode the train to the provincial capital of Tsinan. There he became one of some hundred students at the First Provincial Middle School on Chai-yuan (Examination Hall) Street. Fifty of the students were ranked in four classes or grades and the remaining fifty, including Chiang Kuei, were in the preparatory phase and after a year's work would enter the first year of study.

Student life in Tsinan was stimulating. The school work was not demanding, except for the hated subject of mathematics, and the city offered many diversions. Near the school on Chai-yuan Street were many small restaurants which catered to the students where one could buy a meal, including meat and fish, for a few cents. There were excursions to Thousand Buddha Mountain, outings on Ta-ming Lake, and visits to the Winding Stream Pavillion for tea. In addition, there were opera performances, often featuring renowned beauties of the time, and his first visit to a movie house.

It was as a Middle School student in Tsinan that Chiang Kuei read Lu Hsün's collection of short stories entitled *Na-han* (The Outcry), which appeared in 1923. It would be difficult to overestimate the importance of Chou Shu-jen (1881–1936), who wrote under the pen name of Lu Hsün. A social critic whose weapon was his pen, he attacked the vice and hypocrisy of Chinese society with a concise and restrained but acidly satirical style. *The Outcry,* his first published collection of short stories, contained his most famous stories, including "Diary of a Madman," "K'ung I-chi," and "The True Story of Ah Q."

Chiang Kuei also discovered Kuo Mo-jo's translation of Goethe's romantic novel *The Sorrows of Young Werther.* "I read these two books, and realized that there was a land of literature beyond the old fiction, and all at once heaven and earth were broadened out." But neither of these works made as profound an impression on him as did a translation of *Resurrection,* Leo Tolstoy's tale of a Russian aristocrat's regenerating love for a noble prostitute. It affected him as deeply as the death-scene of Lin Tai-yü, the heroine of Ts'ao Hsüeh-ch'in's *Dream of the Red Chamber*. Many years later, in writing *The Whirlwind*, Chiang Kuei had one of his characters say: "No matter how good de Maupassant's 'The Diamond Necklace' may be, it doesn't have the depth of emotion of Tolstoy's *Resurrection*. After I read 'The Diamond Necklace,' I only thought about it for a few minutes, and then forgot about it. After reading *Resurrection*, I was uncomfortable for several days."[1] It was then that Chiang Kuei began to consider trying his own hand at writing. His first effort, an essay on student life, was accepted and published by the student magazine operated by the Shanghai Commercial Press, China's largest publishing house.

Lectures offered him the opportunity to hear some of the leading intellectual figures of the time. At the First Provincial Middle School, Dr. Hu Shih spoke; this was Chiang Kuei's first sight of the man who set off the vernacular movement in Chinese literature. At the Provincial Assembly Hall, he heard lectures by Professor Ts'ai Yuan-p'ei, the Chancellor of Peking University and a champion of liberal education, and by the Indian poet Rabindranath Tagore.

IV *Communism and First Love*

The only troublesome aspect of Chiang Kuei's student days in Tsinan was his enforced association with his sixth uncle, Wang Hsiang-ch'ien. This individual, who was one of China's earliest Communists, had an important, though largely negative, influence upon Chiang Kuei's youth. Many years later, when Chiang Kuei wrote *The Whirlwind*, he made his sixth uncle the central character and portrayed him with affection and understanding while condemning his political views.

Wang Hsiang-ch'ien (his given name was Ming-ch'iu; Hsiang-ch'ien was his *tzu*) was the eldest son of Wang Yün-p'u, the master of Lucky Star Hall. His younger brother was Wang Chen-ch'ien; both men belonged to the generation of Chiang Kuei's father. In his youth, Wang Hsiang-ch'ien frequented brothels, but before long he put aside that kind of dissipation and became a gourmet. His passion for good eating led him to write a book entitled *Jan-weng shih-p'u* (The Oldster's Cookbook) and have it privately printed for circulation among his friends.

Wang Hsiang-ch'ien received his higher education at the *Pei-*

ching ts'e-hsüeh-kuan (Peking Translation Institute). The Chinese government, under pressure from the Western nations, had established a ministry of foreign affairs in 1861 and this organization, known as the Tsungli Yamen, had in turn established the *T'ung-wen-kuan* (Interpreters' College) to train translators and interpreters. After 1900, this institution was known as the Peking Translation Institute and by that time it had become part of the Imperial University established in 1898 by the Kuang-hsü emperor. After the fall of the Ch'ing Dynasty, this institution was known as National Peking University and it became a center of intellectual life and intense nationalism.

Wang Hsiang-ch'ien studied the German language at the Peking Translation Institute and one of his fellow students was the future Governor of Shantung, Sun Pao-ch'i of Chekiang Province. Sun Pao-ch'i admired Wang Hsiang-ch'ien's talents, and later on, when he was appointed to the governorship, he wrote to his old classmate inviting him to join the provincial administration as a highly placed adviser. But Wang Hsiang-ch'ien did not respond.

Wang Hsiang-ch'ien was a rebel against the conventions of the traditional society even before he became a Marxist. Before reaching the age of thirty, he affected a goatee, and wore spectacles to correct his nearsightedness. At that time such actions were reserved to members of the older generations. Moreover, these gestures were made several years before the May Fourth Movement of 1919, which serves as a watershed between the social conservatism of the old society and the radical individualism and nationalism of the new.

The May Fourth Movement was an explosion of Chinese nationalism set off by the disappointment of China's hopes at the Versailles Treaty conference in Paris. Thousands of high school and college students marched in Peking demanding the return of the Shantung port of Tsingtao which had been leased by Germany in 1898, seized by Japan in 1914, and awarded to Japan by the Western powers in Paris in 1919. The movement spread from Peking to Shanghai and then to all major cities in China. It involved not only students, but merchants and workers as well, and although it did not achieve its immediate political goal, it did awaken millions of Chinese to the reality of their national weakness and humiliation.

The New Culture Movement began before the May Fourth Movement and continued after it. It was inspired by intellectuals who believed that political change was superficial unless preceded by cultural change and it called for the rejection of traditional society and its Confucian value system.

Wang Hsiang-ch'ien came home to Hsiang-chou in the summer of 1920, carrying with him the New Culture Movement's critique of traditional ways. He erected a stage on the exercise ground of the Hsiang-chou Primary School in order to produce three one-act plays. These were "new plays" entitled *The Great Event of a Lifetime* (i.e., marriage), *Returning Home* (the new bride's customary visit to her family shortly after marriage), and *A Blind Man Tells Fortunes*. The point of each play was to attack the institution of arranged marriage and to advocate freedom of choice in marriage.

As local custom did not permit asking girls to play the feminine roles in these plays, the roles were filled by boys and Wang Hsiang-ch'ien decided that Chiang Kuei should play the role of the bride's younger sister in *Returning Home*. In this play, the bride returns home after her marriage and tells her unmarried younger sister of the wrongs she has suffered in her new home.

However, Chiang Kuei absolutely refused to play the role of a girl and when pressed by his uncle, finally resorted to tears. His father and mother, and his adoptive mother as well, took his side and Wang Hsiang-ch'ien had to seek another actor.

The presentation of these three plays in Hsiang-chou attracted a large audience; many of the older women who seldom ventured from their inner quarters turned out to attend the performance. Years later, looking back on this event, Chiang Kuei saw in it the first sign of things to come.

This affair was the first bomb thrown by Mr. Hsiang-ch'ien at the ancestral society of Hsiang-chou. And it was the first drop of foam from the waves of the May Fourth New Culture Movement to reach this small town.[2]

The question of how and why Wang Hsiang-ch'ien came to adopt Marxism cannot be answered with certainty. But as an educated and intelligent man, he certainly was aware of the political, economic, social, and cultural crises through which China was passing and he could observe, within his own clan, the decadence and futility of the old ways. No doubt his rebellious streak of individualism had something to do with it and he may well have been inspired by the Russian revolution of 1917 and the triumph of the Bolsheviks over domestic opposition and foreign intervention. Scholars have suggested that for many Chinese intellectuals the comprehensive Marxist-Leninist philosophy provided an acceptable replacement for the comprehensive Confucian world-view which they had rejected.

Li Ta-chao, China's first important Marxist, was appointed chief librarian and professor of economics at National Peking University in 1918 and it was he who introduced his young assistant librarian, Mao Tse-tung, to Marxism. By the latter months of 1918, Li Ta-chao was well on his way to accepting Marxism and had organized a study group called the Marxist Research Society. Later, in March 1920, Li Ta-chao served as a sort of faculty adviser to a group known as the Peking Society for the Study of Marxist Theory. After the Chinese Communist Party was founded in 1921, Li Ta-chao was one of its guiding spirits until his arrest and execution.

Wang Hsiang-ch'ien was employed as a correspondence secretary at the Provincial Law and Administration School in Tsinan and his activities in that city, in the early nineteen-twenties, imitated those of Professor Li Ta-chao in Peking. Wang Hsiang-ch'ien organized his Society for the Study of Marxist Theory in Tsinan probably in the latter part of 1920 or in 1921. This group seems to have been in existence when Chiang Kuei arrived in Tsinan in 1921, but it cannot have been in existence very long since it had only six or seven members.

The members of this early Marxist group were the two Wang brothers, who were printers and the only workers in the group, Teng En-ming, who was a student at the First Provincial Middle School, Wang Shui-chün, a student at the Provincial Normal School, and Wang Hsiang-ch'ien's daughter Wang Pien, a student at the Girls' Normal School. The only member of this group whose existence can be verified by a source other than Chiang Kuei's reminiscences is Teng En-ming. Mao Tse-tung, in a conversation with the American reporter Edgar Snow, mentioned Teng En-ming and Wang Chin-mei as early members of the Communist Party in Tsinan and Wang Chin-mei is probably the Wang Shui-chün mentioned by Chiang Kuei.

Wang Hsiang-ch'ien was the senior member of the Wang clan resident in Tsinan and as such he was in charge of his nephew. Chiang Kuei had been brought up in a traditional household and taught to obey his elders. Thus, although he had been able, with the support of his parents, to avoid playing the role of a girl in Wang Hsiang-ch'ien's play in Hsiang-chou, in Tsinan his uncle succeeded in forcing him to play that very role in the same play at the Yün-ying Middle School. By the same token, when Wang Hsiang-ch'ien required him to attend the meetings of the Society for the Study of Marxist Theory, Chiang Kuei obeyed.

The Society met every week or ten days at the offices of the Educational Association, at the guest house of the Yün-ying Middle School, or aboard rowboats on Ta-ming Lake. Chiang Kuei had no interest whatever in the Society but he dutifully attended the meetings. Marxist theory was discussed at these meetings, although if Chiang Kuei's fictional portrait of the group in the first chapter of *The Whirlwind* is accurate, they had only the sketchiest understanding of Marxism. However, they did not merely discuss theory. They at least considered developing an organization in the Yü-feng Cotton Mills at Lo-k'ou near Tsinan.

On one occasion, Teng En-ming suggested that Chiang Kuei be inducted and become a "party member." But Wang Hsiang-ch'ien immediately vetoed the suggestion with the remark that Chiang Kuei's academic performance was too poor.

Chiang Kuei's association with his sixth uncle cost him not only the time spent at the fortnightly meetings but also a good deal of his money. Normally, he would have been well off because his adopted mother provided him with a hundred dollars a month and his own father furnished him with a like sum. But Wang Hsiang-ch'ien's party activities were costly and when he ran out of his own money, he frequently borrowed from his nephew and did not bother to repay.

At length, dissatisfied with Chiang Kuei's scholastic work, Wang Hsiang-ch'ien came to believe that a sojourn in the Soviet Union would provide his nephew with the necessary discipline. Wang Hsiang-ch'ien had sent his own daughter, Wang Pien, off to the Soviet Union. He also prevailed upon his younger brother, Wang Chen-ch'ien, to allow his son Wang Mao-chien, who had not yet

of speech.

Chiang Kuei was fifteen at the time; Chin-tzu was perhaps thirteen. They saw each other frequently after that and began to meet
briefly in the small courtyard outside the *Ts'ui-mai-ch'ang* for late-
evening trysts. Before long, they were discussing marriage.

Chin-tzu asked Chiang Kuei to request his older companion
Meng to approach her mother as a go-between and bring up the
matter of marriage. When Chiang Kuei spoke to Meng, Meng
thought the idea unlikely. The girl was on the verge of what promised to be a rewarding career and her mother would be unwilling to
let her marry. Even if the mother were willing, she would certainly
demand a great deal of money. Chiang Kuei recognized the logic in
this but insisted that Meng approach the girl's mother and strangely
enough, the mother consented. She preferred an orthodox marriage
for her daughter rather than an income from her performances.
Even the customary gifts from the groom's family to the bride's
might be dispensed with.

When Chiang Kuei learned of this favorable reply, he wrote to
his father at once and asked him to come to Tsinan to arrange for
the marriage. After a few days, his father's reply came and it was
decisively negative. Furious, the fifteen-year-old Chiang Kuei
bought a sleeping-berth ticket on a steamer to Shanghai and
Hangchow and fled Tsinan. At Hangchow, a city regarded as the
most scenic and beautiful in China, he boarded another boat to sail
up the Ch'ien-t'ang River to Chin-hua.

Chiang Kuei had never cared for writing poetry and his reluctance had often frustrated his teachers. However, as he sailed
toward Chin-hua, his own emotions and the beauty of the
September scene prompted him to write a poem. After much effort,
he produced a four-line poem with seven characters to each line and
a rhyme-scheme of A A B C.

> Dreams broken, the water of Twin Dragon Spring is sweet
> Ninth Sister tarries awhile at Ch'ien-t'ang
> A single sail bears the warriors to the attack
> But before the sky is cold the heart is chilled.[3]

At Chin-hua in Chekiang Province, Chiang Kuei's money ran out
and he had to return to Hsiang-chou. When he showed his poem to

his cousin, Second Brother, the latter accused him of having plagiarized it from an ancient poet but would not say from which one. Chiang Kuei was irritated by this unjust criticism because he had composed the poem entirely by himself. But upon reflection, he realized that, given the antiquity of China's poetic tradition, it was virtually impossible to write a wholly original poem, for whatever one's poetic intention, chances were that it had been anticipated long ago. This sense of living under the weight of past generations, at least in the sphere of poetry, seems to have remained in Chiang Kuei's mind. Years later when he wrote the novel *Breaking Free*, he expressed such an observation through the words of the character who represented himself. Probably this is one reason why Chiang Kuei addressed himself to the novel instead of poetry.

Chiang Kuei did not return to Tsinan. Instead, he transferred to the Chiao-ao Middle School in Tsingtao. The probable reason for this transfer was because his natural parents and his adoptive mother did not wish him to remain in the same city with the singing-girl Chin-tzu. From Chiang Kuei's point of view, the transfer was a way to escape the influence of his sixth uncle Wang Hsiang-ch'ien's Marxism.

The Chiao-ao Middle School in Tsingtao where Chiang Kuei enrolled in the fall of 1924 was operated by the Kuomintang and soon Chiang Kuei joined the Kuomintang. Although this involvement in revolutionary political activity was not typical for youth of his generation within the Wang clan—apparently none of his brothers followed his example—Chiang Kuei's particular background made such a course very likely. When he became the adopted son of the martyred revolutionary Wang Ming-shao, Chiang Kuei inherited his late uncle's commitment. The T'ung Meng Hui had ceased to exist after the establishment of the Chinese Republic in 1912 but the Kuomintang was its successor organization and many of the T'ung Meng Hui revolutionaries continued their careers in the Kuomintang. Miss Jen had often admonished Chiang Kuei to remember that his fifth uncle had belonged to the "*Mintang*" (People's Party, an early synonym for the revolutionary party). Moreover, his association with Wang Hsiangch'ien must have awakened him to the world of revolutionary politics and when he had entered the First Provincial Middle School in Tsinan, his guarantor had been Wang Lo-p'ing, an active

Kuomintang member who edited the party's newspaper in Tsinan.

The first Kuomintang, as already mentioned, was a political party founded in 1912 to wage its political struggles in the newly established Parliament of the Republic. Although it gained a plurality of seats in the first parliamentary elections in 1913, the machinations of President Yuan Shih-k'ai and the rivalry of other political parties prevented it from accomplishing much. The abortive "Second Revolution of 1913"—the rebellion of three provincial governors affiliated with the Kuomintang—afforded Yuan Shih-k'ai an excuse for outlawing the Kuomintang and purging its members from the Parliament.

Dr. Sun Yat-sen had not been active in the Kuomintang. After the failure of the Second Revolution, he found himself once again in exile. He established another revolutionary party, the *Chung-kuo ko-ming-tang* (Chinese Revolutionary Party), in 1914 to struggle against the dictatorship of Yuan Shih-k'ai.

Yuan Shih-k'ai attempted, in 1915, to restore the imperial system with himself as the first emperor. But widespread opposition and a rebellion in south China caused him to abandon the attempt and he died in 1916. After Yuan's death, China fell prey to the warlords. These rapacious military commanders, many of whom had risen to power in Yuan Shih-k'ai's Northern Army, subjected China to twelve years of misrule.

In 1919, in the wake of the May Fourth Movement, Dr. Sun Yat-sen founded yet another revolutionary organization, the *Chung-kuo kuo-min-tang* (Chinese Nationalist Party) referred to hereafter as the Kuomintang. For a time, Dr. Sun Yat-sen headed a government in Canton which challenged the legitimacy of the warlord-dominated regime in Peking. However, the Peking regime was recognized by all foreign powers as the established government of the Chinese Republic.

Between 1919 and 1923, the Kuomintang achieved little. It was less a modern political party than a loose collection of revolutionary politicians bound only by personal loyalty to Dr. Sun Yat-sen and it was forced to rely for military support upon southern warlords of questionable loyalty.

In 1922, the Communist Third International, or Comintern, began to make overtures to Dr. Sun Yat-sen as the leader of the major revolutionary party in China. Conversations held between various Comintern agents and Dr. Sun culminated in the Sun-Joffe joint manifesto of January 1923. This document proclaimed the agreement of both parties that the conditions did not exist in China for the establishment of the Soviet system, let alone Communism, that the main tasks facing China were the attainment of national unification, which meant getting rid of the warlords, and national independence, which meant getting rid of the imperialists, and that in carrying out these tasks the Chinese could count on the fraternal aid of the Soviet Union.

The Chinese Communist Party was founded in July 1921. By the time of the second Party Congress in 1922, the Communist leaders, prompted by the Comintern, had decided upon a policy of cooperation with Dr. Sun Yat-sen's Kuomintang. In size and prestige the Kuomintang was clearly the leading revolutionary organization in China and its goals of national unification and national independence were shared by the Communist Party. Therefore, Communist Party members would enter the Kuomintang as individuals, while retaining their Communist Party membership. The Communist Party retained its own separate organizational entity and of course maintained its own revolutionary program, which went far beyond that of the Kuomintang.

The Kuomintang was reorganized in 1924 along the organizational lines of the Communist Party of the Soviet Union. At the first National Congress of this reorganized Kuomintang, held in Canton in January 1924, the Three Great Policies of alignment with the Soviet Union in foreign affairs, collaboration with the Chinese Communist Party in domestic affairs, and the creation of a base of mass support among the workers and peasants were adopted. Chinese Communists were allotted seats on the Central Executive Committee. The Whampoa Military Academy was established on an island near Canton to train the cadres of the new revolutionary army. Michael Borodin arrived as the Comintern's political adviser to the Kuomintang and a host of Soviet military advisers came to offer their Chinese hosts the fund of Soviet revolutionary experience and expertise.

This reorganized Kuomintang was a far more effective revolutionary instrument than any of Dr. Sun Yat-sen's earlier organizations. But before he could wield this weapon, he died on March 12, 1925. In his last testament, he urged his comrades to carry on the unfinished struggle. After Dr. Sun's death, a contest for power took place among the leaders of the Kuomintang. The conservatives feared Soviet and Chinese Communist influence and the specter of social revolution. The Left Kuomintang faction wished to maintain the policies established in 1924.

Such was the political situation at the time of Chiang Kuei's entry into the Kuomintang. Almost at once, the sixteen-year-old youth was confronted with the violent issues of the day. In the winter and spring of 1925, a wave of strikes, some economic in origin and others inspired by patriotic and nationalistic feelings, took place in many Chinese cities.

In April 1925, workers of the Kiaochow-Tsinan Railway General Labor Union in Tsingtao helped the workers at the Japanese-owned Ta-k'ang Cotton Mill organize a union. A strike followed, involving twelve thousand workers, and although the Japanese government sent reinforcements of police to Tsingtao, the strike was not ended for three weeks. The strikers, who had received large sums of money from local students and other organizations, gained many of their economic demands. However, the matter did not rest there. The Japanese factory owners asked the municipal authorities to persuade the union to disband. When persuasion failed, the Chinese authorities arrested the union leaders on May 25, 1925. A riot resulted. Workers occupied and wrecked the mill. On the night of May 28, 1925, the workers were attacked by Chinese marines and armed police. Eight workers were killed, ten seriously wounded, and seventy arrested.

Two days after the suppression of the cotton mill workers' strike in Tsingtao, the May Thirtieth Incident took place in Shanghai. The May Thirtieth Incident was the shooting of thirteen Chinese demonstrators by Shanghai Municipal Police under British officers. News of the Tsingtao killings added to the fury aroused in Shanghai by May Thirtieth, and in the same manner, after May Thirtieth a wave of outrage traveled back up the coast to Tsingtao.

The municipal authorities in Tsingtao permitted demonstrations in connection with the May Thirtieth Incident but the demonstrators were not permitted to mention the similar incident which had just taken place in Tsingtao. Despite this restriction, workers and students organized and protested. In the tense atmosphere of the nationwide drive against imperialism, it was not long before another incident took place. A boy worker was beaten in a factory and workers at three cotton mills walked out on strike on July 24, 1925.

On July 25, the second day of the strike, the Military Governor of Shantung, General Chang Tsung-ch'ang, arrived in Tsingtao. Chang Tsung-ch'ang, who had assumed the post of Military Governor only the month before, was a gross giant of a man who had earned a reputation as one of the most picturesque and savage of the northern warlords. He promptly suppressed the labor and the anti-imperialist movements, arrested many workers, and executed an editor and a teacher who were considered agitators. Tsingtao, in the words of the Communist historian Hua Kang, became "a world of terror."

What part Chiang Kuei may have taken in the student anti-imperialist movement in Tsingtao remains to be discovered although as a member of the Kuomintang almost certainly he was involved to some extent. Overt revolutionary activity in Tsingtao would have been risky at best, but in the south the Kuomintang was gathering itself for the Northern Expedition. At this point, when he was eighteen years old, his feelings may well have been those which he put into the mind of the young protagonist of his novel *The Two Suns:*

Hung T'ung-yeh gazed at the vastness of river and sky, and felt that such a lovely country really had great possibilities. And the first step, the first step that must be taken, was to get rid of the power of the foreigners, and knock down imperialism. In order to knock down imperialism, it would be necessary first to wipe out the warlords within the country who depended upon imperialism. He thought, these two slogans put forward by Mr. Sun Chung-shan's Kuomintang completely meet the demands of the people of the nation. The tide was rising, and it must achieve its goal; there was no question about that.[4]

In 1926, Chiang Kuei and a few like-minded friends left Tsingtao and ran off to Canton, headquarters of the Kuomintang, to take part in the revolution.

CHAPTER 2

Revolution and War

I   Revolution and Reaction

PROBABLY Chiang Kuei and his companions arrived in Canton in the late spring of 1926. His first days in the ancient city must have nearly overwhelmed him with a variety of striking impressions: the oppressive moist heat of the south, the swarming boat people on their sampans, the unfamiliar dress and manners of the Cantonese, the strange sounds of the Kwangtung dialect, unintelligibly different from the Mandarin of the north, and above all the sense of being where great events were taking place. Canton was the headquarters of the Kuomintang's revolutionary effort. The great strike and boycott that had paralyzed Hong Kong and the foreign settlement on Shameen Island since June 1925 was still in effect and preparations were underway for the Northern Expedition.

Chiang Kuei must have seen many workers' pickets in Canton, and later on in Wuhan, for they were present in considerable numbers and performed many functions. When the Hong Kong strike and boycott began in 1925, about one hundred thousand strikers moved to Canton, where they lived by the assistance of the government and by contributions from sympathizers throughout China. From their ranks were recruited about two thousand pickets organized in five units. The workers' pickets enforced the strike and boycott of Hong Kong and of Shameen Island and tried violators in a strikers' court. In their dark blue uniforms, bearing arms or staves, they were a common sight on the streets of Canton.

Few foreigners were to be seen. The Soviet advisers, when not on duty in the various party, government, and military offices, kept to their quarters as a matter of policy. Nearly all of the Westerners had withdrawn by that time; those who remained were on Shameen

Island across a small canal from the Shakee Road embankment. Shameen Island in 1926 was a sepulchral place, supplied by ship from Hong Kong, guarded by British soldiers, cut off from Chinese Canton by a wall of hostility. Across the canal, a small monument on the Shakee Road embankment bearing the inscription "Do Not Forget This Day" recalled the massacre of June 23, 1925. On that day, British and French machine-gunners on Shameen Island had opened fire on a demonstrating procession of workers, students, military cadets, and Boy Scouts passing along Shakee Road. Fifty-two were killed and one hundred seventeen wounded.

Chiang Kuei had come to Canton to take part in the work of the Kuomintang's Central Youth Bureau. His duties were those of any Youth Bureau member: to stir up the youth in support of the Kuomintang's two main goals of destroying the warlords and driving off the imperialists. It is generally acknowledged that the rapid progress of the National Revolutionary Army on the Northern Expedition was made possible by the effective work of the propaganda teams which preceded the military forces and aroused the people to welcome and support them. Kuo Mo-jo, the poet and scholar, who traveled to Hankow in 1926 with the army's General Political Department, found that the people in villages which the army had not even reached were familiar with the idea that the National Revolutionary Army was different from the northern army of General Wu P'ei-fu and was on the side of the people.

The Northern Expedition, which was meant to defeat the armies of the various northern warlords and unify China, was launched in July 1926. Chiang Kai-shek, one of several men who were maneuvering for control of the Kuomintang, was appointed Commander-in-Chief of the National Revolutionary Army.

The triple cities of Wuhan (Hankow, Hanyang, and Wuchang) were the first major targets of the Northern Expedition. Hanyang surrendered on September 26, 1926, and Hankow was occupied on the following day.

Wuchang, however, defied several desperate assaults and held out for more than a month. The commander, Liu Yü-ch'ün, apparently convinced that his master Wu P'ei-fu would return in triumph, held stubbornly on to the city. Airplanes piloted by Russians flew over Wuchang and dropped leaflets. But the National Revolutionary Army had no heavy artillery and the ancient walls

and iron-bound gates of Wuchang held firm. In the end, it was
hunger which opened the city. By the fourth week of the siege, the
two hundred thousand people within the walls of Wuchang were
beginning to starve. They ate roots, bark, dogs, cats, rats, and a sort
of earthen dumpling mixed with chaff. The defending soldiers existed on one or two bowls of rice gruel a day and had no tobacco.
On October 3, Liu Yü-ch'ün agreed that civilians might leave the
city and two people were crushed to death as the crowds surged
through the gate. Eventually Liu Yü-ch'ün saw the futility of his
resolution and capitulated. Wuchang was given up to the National
Revolutionary Army on October 10, 1926.

Before long, the Kuomintang political leaders left Canton and
assembled in Wuhan, which was declared the capital of the
National Government of China on January 1, 1927. Many of the
leading members of this government belonged to the "Left
Kuomintang." They believed that the Kuomintang should incite
and lead a social revolution supported by mass organizations of
workers and peasants and they were willing to accept the help of
the Communists.

The Right, or conservative, faction of the Kuomintang was not so
well represented in the Wuhan government but many of the officers
of the National Revolutionary Army belonged to this group. The
Right Kuomintang feared social revolution and wished to concentrate upon the military unification of China, while taking a cautious
approach to the foreign powers and their interests. They distrusted
the mass organizations and were alarmed by the rapidly expanding
influence of the Chinese Communist Party.

Chiang Kuei, as a worker in the Central Youth Bureau of the
Kuomintang, followed the government to Wuhan. He lived in
Hankow for seven or eight months, probably from January to July
or August of 1927, or from the inauguration of the government in
the new capital to the break between the government and the Communist Party. During this time, he saw revolutionary politics at first
hand and accumulated the experiences upon which he was later to
draw in writing *The Two Suns*.

Wuhan in 1927, like Canton in 1926, was a city in which the
everyday tenor of life was disrupted, for better or worse, by politics.
It was the political center of the ongoing National Revolution.
Michael Borodin, the Comintern adviser, was there as was Soong

Ch'ing-ling, the widow of the late Dr. Sun Yat-sen. The streets were full of uniforms, demonstrations, parades, and slogans. Foreign warships rode at anchor on the Yangtze River and a stream of foreign missionaries, recalled from their stations in the hinterland, passed through Wuhan on their way downriver to the safety of Shanghai. Meanwhile, on the streets and wharves of Wuhan and in the fields of Hunan Province, the rising demands of the workers and peasants whose hopes had been aroused by the Communists and the Kuomintang placed an intolerable strain upon the alliance between the two parties.

The organized militancy of the Wuhan working class, supported by propaganda which told them that a new government representing them was now in power and that a new order was beginning, led to a wave of strikes. In the winter of 1926 and the spring of 1927, Wuhan workers in the post office, in printing plants, cotton mills, cigarette factories, banks, shops, and handicraft industries struck.

In the countryside too the old order was violently disrupted. Mao Tse-tung, who had worked to organize the peasants in his native province of Hunan, saw his efforts succeed. By January 1927, the peasant associations counted some two million members, and since each membership usually represented a household, could claim some ten million followers. These peasant associations attacked the landlords and their hirelings, ousted corrupt officials, established popular courts to try and punish offenders, and challenged all traditional customs and institutions. Mao Tse-tung's classic report on the peasant movement in Hunan left no doubt of the violent character of this rural social revolution.

The leaders of the Wuhan government seemed not to have been prepared for what happened when the people took their slogans seriously. Two days after the establishment of the government, a great demonstration took place before the British Concession in Hankow. Successive demonstrations on the following days led to the bloodless occupation of the British Concession by Chinese crowds. On January 6, 1927, the British Concession in Kiukiang, downriver from Wuhan, was occupied and reclaimed in the same manner. The British response was to ratify through a diplomatic agreement what had already taken place.

During the month of February 1927, organized labor gave further proofs of its new-found strength in the Wuhan cities. On February

24, the largest demonstration ever held in Hankow took place. The General Labor Union, which had been organized by the Communists immediately after the surrender of Wuchang, called a twenty-four-hour strike, and a mass meeting was followed by a parade which took an hour and a half to pass a given point. Four days later a one-hour general strike was called to protest the presence of British troops in Shanghai. This strike was enforced by the workers' pickets and all traffic, including rickshas, was stopped. In March, two newspapers regarded as unfriendly, the American *Hankow Herald* and the British *Central China Post,* were forced to shut down when the union pulled their Chinese workers off the job. Picketing began at all foreign banks in Hankow on March 21, and the British and French banks, considering their employees' demands for higher wages exorbitant, shut their doors.

The militancy of the labor unions frightened Chinese and foreign capital from Wuhan and economic conditions swiftly grew critical. The currency issued by the government's Central Bank was discounted at thirty percent and went lower every day. By June 1927, there were 120,000 unemployed workers. The government, facing bankruptcy, took steps to curb the labor unions and denounced many of their demands as unreasonable and excessive. In the countryside too the government acted to put a stop to what it felt were the excesses of the peasant associations. In short, the Left Kuomintang, the Chinese Communist Party, and the National Government in which they collaborated were alike confused and upset by the demands of the masses which their own propaganda had helped to arouse.

The first six months of 1927 must have been very exciting ones for Chiang Kuei. The English poet Wordsworth wrote of the early days of the French Revolution, "Bliss was it in that dawn to be alive / And to be young was very heaven." Chiang Kuei was nineteen and in the midst of a revolution even more profound than the French. He could not have been aware of the confused maneuverings and compromises of the government and party leaders. Probably for him the first part of the year was a time of great expectations and the summer a time of growing apprehension. He must have heard in April 1927 of ominous events taking place elsewhere in China. In Peking, military police of the warlord Chang Tso-lin raided the Soviet Russian embassy on April 6. Among those arrested in the raid was Professor Li Ta-chao, one of the founders of the Chinese Communist Party. Three weeks later, on April 27, Li Ta-chao was executed by strangulation.

In Shanghai, the organized workers arose on March 21, 1927, and after fierce fighting defeated the troops of the Shantung warlord Chang Tsung-ch'ang. Even his ferocious White Russian mercenaries were routed. Having secured Shanghai except for the International Settlement and the French Concession, the workers opened the city to the advancing National Revolutionary Army forces led by Chiang Kai-shek. It is generally considered that after his arrival in Shanghai, Chiang Kai-shek gained financial support which enabled him to do without Soviet aid and the support of the mass organizations. On April 12, 1927, Chiang Kai-shek moved with speed and ruthlessness against the organized and armed workers of Shanghai. His troops, assisted by the Shanghai gangster societies, crushed the workers within a few days and hundreds, perhaps thousands, were slaughtered. His coup relieved the anxieties of many Chinese and foreigners alike, and indicated with brutal clarity his future course.

In Wuhan, the Central Executive Committee of the Kuomintang reacted by expelling Chiang Kai-shek from the party and depriving him of all official positions. But this was an empty gesture, for Chiang Kai-shek had his own version of the Kuomintang and his own government in Nanking.

Disturbing news came to Wuhan of the spreading reaction which was being imposed in city after city to the east. In Wuhan the atmosphere changed too. The government adopted a friendlier attitude toward foreigners so that by April 26 the easing tension was noticeable to an American diplomatic observer. The *Hankow Herald*, shut down in March, was allowed to resume publication by the end of April.

Yet, if the tension was easing from an American point of view, it was increasing from the point of view of the Left Kuomintang and the Communist Party. On May 16, General Hsia Tou-yin rebelled against the Wuhan government and advanced toward the capital. Along his line of march, officials of the peasant associations who fell into his hands were tortured and killed. Hsia Tou-yin's advance was halted not far from Wuhan. Only a few days later came the news of the "Ma-jih" Incident on May 21, 1927. General Hsü K'o-hsiang, whose regiment was responsible for Changsha, the capital of Hunan Province, had rebelled and wiped out the Communists and the peasant organizations in and around that city.

Wang Ching-wei, a longtime rival of Chiang Kai-shek within the Kuomintang, had returned from his voluntary exile in France in April 1927 to assume the chairmanship of the Wuhan government. He attempted to outmaneuver Chiang Kai-shek with the military help of General Feng Yü-hsiang, but the attempt failed when Feng advised him to seek a rapprochement with Chiang Kai-shek. At this point, the Chinese Communist Party leaders received a telegram from Stalin ordering them to prepare a massive armed insurrection, involving seizing control of the government and the Kuomintang in Wuhan. Wang Ching-wei was shown this telegram by the Indian Comintern agent M. N. Roy and it influenced him to break with the Communists sooner than he otherwise might have done. The Communists were expelled from posts in the Kuomintang and the Wuhan government toward the end of July 1927. But the government itself was on the verge of collapse. Soong Ch'ing-ling, a living symbol of revolutionary legitimacy as the widow of Dr. Sun Yat-sen, left China, as did Michael Borodin, in July. Most of the Communists departed to seek refuge in Kiangsi Province. As Chiang Kuei put it in The Whirlwind, "the tree of the Wuhan regime fell and the monkeys scattered."[1]

The Communist military uprising at Nanchang, the capital of Kiangsi Province, on August 1, 1927, made the break between the Left Kuomintang and the Communists irreparable. The Wuhan government began to suppress the revolutionaries and the mass organizations as ruthlessly as had Chiang Kai-shek. During the first part of August, an American diplomatic observer noted that eight Communists had been executed during the week in Hankow, and this figure probably represented only the tip of the iceberg. By August 20, the National Government as it had existed in Wuhan was no more, and the capital of China was Nanking.

The following ten years, 1927 to 1937, are often referred to as the "Nanking Decade." The National Government in Nanking ruled China, the Kuomintang ruled the National Government, and Chiang Kai-shek ruled the Kuomintang. Chiang's control was far from absolute for he had to balance rival factions within the Kuomintang against one another and certain provinces remained under the control of former warlords whose obedience to Nanking was conditional. Still, during the Nanking Decade, China enjoyed a greater degree of unity than it had known since the fall of the Ch'ing Dynasty in 1911.

A certain amount of progress was achieved during the Nanking Decade, but this progress was most noticeable in the cities and in the modern sectors of the economy. The truly crucial problem, that of the hundreds of millions of peasants, was not effectively dealt with and probably could not have been short of the kind of revolution advocated by the Communists.

As for the Communists, they had been defeated in 1927 but not totally destroyed. Their grip upon the cities was broken but they survived here and there in the countryside, and on the Hunan-Kiangsi border small bands led by Mao Tse-tung and Chu Teh formed a nucleus of Communist strength in the early nineteen-thirties.

II Marriage and Writing

When Chiang Kuei began to write the story of the Wuhan episode, he tried and rejected two titles before his final choice, The Two Suns. This title referred to the two parties which had competed for control of the revolution. By the time of the nineteen-year-old Chiang Kuei's departure from Wuhan in August 1927, the Communist sun was in eclipse and the twelve rays of the Kuomintang sun shone triumphantly over China.

The flag of the Republic of China, from 1928 onward, bore the Kuomintang party emblem, a twelve-rayed white sun on a blue canton, in the upper left hand quarter of a red ground. This flag was raised in Nanking, the first capital of the Ming Dynasty, capital of the Taiping rebels in the mid-nineteenth century, and the first capital of the Provisional Government of the Republic of China in 1911, on April 18, 1927. Peking, capital of the northern warlord regimes, fell to the warlords Feng Yü-hsiang and Yen Hsi-shan, who had aligned themselves with the Kuomintang. Finally, Chang Hsüeh-liang, the young warlord of Manchuria, signaled his allegiance to the Nanking government when he raised its flag over Mukden on December 29, 1928.

Yet the formal national unity symbolized by the flag was superficial and frequently broken by provincial and regional secessions and rebellions. Nor was the new government able to alleviate the sufferings imposed by nature. In Chiang Kuei's native Shantung, a famine raged in January 1928, reducing more than four million people to extreme poverty. The famine, brought on by three years of bad crops, a locust pest, and drought, plus high taxes, uncontrolled soldiers, and banditry, brought the price of land down from the pre-famine $90.00 an acre to a low of $4.50 an acre. Desperate parents sold their daughters. The price of young girls sold as concubines and prostitutes ran from approximately $2.00 to $11.50. Often those too young to be sold were killed by their parents. By March, Shantung was reported to be overrun by wild dogs.

Chiang Kuei left Wuhan for the city of Kaifeng in Honan Province. From there he went to Shanghai, China's greatest metropolis and the major outpost of the Western presence in China. It was a bustling but squalid city where, according to Chiang Monlin, Minister of Education in the National Government and later Chancellor of Peking University, both Chinese and Western civilizations were at their worst. Along with the bustle and the squalor were violence and terror as the Kuomintang government and the underground cadres of the Chinese Communist Party waged their merciless war. The large and well-organized criminal Red and Green Gangs contributed to the bloodshed. But the death toll of politics and crime was dwarfed by the death toll of poverty. The poor died like flies in the streets of Shanghai. According to the American journalist Agnes Smedley, the official figures of the Shanghai Municipal Council revealed that from 32,000 to 35,000 dead bodies were picked up in the streets each year and buried in paupers' graves.

But Shanghai was not only an emporium of wealth and the scene of struggles between the Kuomintang and the Chinese Communist Party; it was also the literary capital of China, with its attendant controversy.

The first literary school or group to emerge was *Wen-hsüeh yen-chiu hui* (Literary Research Society). This group was formed by the writers Chou Tso-jen, Chu Hsi-tsu, Keng Chi-chih, Cheng Chen-to, Ch'ü Shih-ying, Wang T'ung-chao (Chiang Kuei's uncle), Mao Tun, Chiang Pai-li, Yeh Shao-chün, Kuo Shao-yü, Sun Fu-yüan, and Hsü Ti-shan. They persuaded the Commercial Press of Shanghai, China's largest publishing firm, to give them editorial control of the journal *Hsiao-shuo yüeh-pao* (Fiction Monthly), which had been in circulation for over a decade, and this control was given to Mao Tun as editor with the January 1921 issue. The manifesto of the Literary Research Society was published in this issue and it proclaimed their serious purpose:

The time when literature was a trifle with which one amused oneself when one felt elated, or passed the time when one was disappointed, is now past. We believe that literature is a kind of work, and moreover that it is a very important kind of work. Those who influence literature ought to make this their life's work, just as with workers and peasants. So we are founding this society, hoping that it will be not only an ordinary literary society, but that it will also become the basis for a union of fellow writers, to plan for the development and consolidation of literary work.[2]

According to Mao Tun, the Literary Research Society was a very loose assocation of writers who had no plans or ambitions in common and agreed only that literature was no longer to be simply an ornament or a consolation. However, he added, some of the members, including Ping Hsin, Wang T'ung-chao, Yeh Shao-chün, and Lo Hua-sheng, felt that literature should reflect social reality and should take a stand on questions affecting human life. This attitude was referred to as "Humane Literature."

The writers of the Literary Research Society also sought to serve the cause of a developing Chinese literature by introducing Western criticism and by providing translations of foreign works, particularly by authors of Russian, French, and northern European origins. Their pioneering journal, *Fiction Monthly,* offered young writers a forum.

In the summer of 1921, a group of young writers who shared an attitude of romanticism and believed in art for art's sake formed the *Ch'uang-tsao she* (Creation Society). This group included Kuo Mo-jo, a poet and translator, Ch'eng Fang-wu, a critic, Chang Tzu-p'ing, a novelist, and Cheng Po-chi, a translator. The public life of the Creation Society began with the publication in 1922 of Kuo Mo-jo's *Shen-nü* (The Goddesses), Yü Ta-fu's *Chen-lun* (Sinking), Kuo Mo-jo's translation of Goethe's *Sorrows of Young Werther,* and

Cheng Po-chi's translation of Remy de Gourmont's *A Night in the Luxembourg*.

Cheng Po-chi wrote of the group:

The Creation Society also styled itself "without an 'ism'," and said: "We began with several friends simply getting together. Our 'isms', our thoughts, weren't the same, and there was no need to demand that they be the same." But next came the explanation: "That which we have in common is basically only the demand of our hearts: to devote ourselves to literary activities."[3]

Cheng Po-chi went on to explain that the Romanticism of the members of the Creation Society was the result of having suffered two painful and alienating experiences: they had lived as poor students in the capitalistic society of Japan and they had been sorely disillusioned upon their return to their own miserable China. During its initial period, from 1921 until 1925, the Creation Society stood for the Romantic ideal of individual liberation from the constraints of a moribund society, and the writings of Yü Ta-fu in particular dealt with the sufferings of sensitive youth. The Communist literary historian Wang Yao explained that the writers of the Creation Society appealed to the youth of that time because they shared feelings of confusion and melancholy.

By 1925, the Creation Society had adopted Marxism and was bringing up the slogan of "Revolutionary Literature." Thereafter, until the dissolution of the society by the government in 1929, many of the original members and their young successors continued to advocate Marxism and revolution in a succession of ephemeral journals and their efforts were quite effective.

Even those literary men who had not yet adopted Marxism were deeply concerned with social questions and with the writer's responsibility to society. Mao Tun wrote:

Still more do we in this time of ours hope that literature can assume the heavy burden of arousing the people and giving them strength; we hope that the literary youth of the country will no longer shut their eyes, imagining themselves in a dream of the Tower of the Seven Precious Things, and forgetting that their bodies are actually in a pigsty, and even more do we absolutely oppose the youth shutting their eyes and forgetting the manacles on their bodies, and even recklessly ridiculing those who are struggling to free themselves of the manacles; that "spiritual victory" method in the style of "Ah Q" is shameful.[4]

It was upon the youth that this burden fell, according to Mao Tun, and he advised aspiring writers to familiarize themselves with their subject matter.

Just now, most of those who are eagerly interested in the new literature are the youth, and the new thought demands that they pay attention to social questions and sympathize with the "injured and the insulted"; they must pour this spirit into their work; however, as a rule they are not very familiar with the living conditions of such people. . . .[5]

Mao Tun, and the Literary Research Society of which he was a leader, continued to advocate a "Humane Literature" based upon sympathy for the oppressed and accurate social observation. Because of Mao Tun's conviction that literature should accurately reflect society even if the reflection did not match the ideas of the revolutionaries, he was attacked by the members of the Creation Society. Lu Hsün, who also upheld an independent role for literature, was likewise the target of polemics.

A third group of writers, including Liang Shih-ch'iu, Hsü Chih-mo, and Hu Shih, drew together around the *Hsin-yüeh* (Crescent Moon Monthly), which appeared in 1928. They advocated the concepts of "health" and "dignity" in thought and word. Liang Shih-ch'iu, in an essay entitled "Literature and Revolution," wrote that "Great literature is founded in a firm and general human life,"[6] and "Human life is the only standard by which to measure literature."[7] Liang Shih-ch'iu also denied that literature possessed a class nature and declared that the question of the relationship between literature and revolution was not worth the effort of clarifying it. Naturally, the Crescent Moon group was also attacked by the Creation Society.

In 1930, the Chinese Communist Party launched an ambitious attempt to capture control of the literary world. Lu Hsün, doyen of the literature of protest, Mao Tun, China's leading novelist, Yü Ta-fu, the advocate of Romantic individualism, Chiang Kuang-tzu, the author of revolutionary novels, and several other literary figures organized the *Chung-kuo tso-lien tso-chia lien-meng* (Chinese Left-wing Writers League) in Shanghai on March 2, 1930. The League, in its manifesto entitled *Outline of Theory,* frankly proclaimed its identification with the Communist revolutionary struggle.

Art, in a period of social change, if it is not to become utterly frozen as a conservative factor, becoming a tool for supporting the obstinate rulers, must press boldly on in a progressive direction, and become a weapon in the struggle for liberation. And only if it marches in the same direction as the progress of history can art spread its glorious light. . . .

Therefore, our art opposes the feudal class, opposes the bourgeoisie, and opposes the tendency of the petty-bourgeoisie to "discard class position." Therefore we cannot but choose to devote ourselves to the production of the art of the proletariat. . . .

In our attitude toward contemporary society we cannot but take part in the liberation movement of the world proletariat, and struggle against the international anti-proletarian reactionary force.[8]

The Chinese Left-wing Writers League was dissolved quietly in 1936 to make way for the "united front" of patriotic literature, just as class struggle was to be subordinated temporarily to national defense.

Chiang Kuei came to Shanghai in 1928 as a nineteen-year-old veteran of the first phase of the Kuomintang-Communist Party cooperation. There he met the woman who was to share his life through war, revolution, and poverty for the next thirty-three years. Miss Yen Hsüeh-mei, daughter of Yen Ch'ang-ling of Shanghai, was two years his senior. She worked at the Pao-lung Hospital in Shanghai. The couple had two things in common: both spoke a little German and both were members of the Anglican Church. Miss Yen, like Chiang Kuei, had been brought up in a non-Christian Chinese household. She had attended a primary school operated by the Anglican Church and had become a convert. Chiang Kuei came by his conversion to the Anglican Church on his own. They became engaged, and Chiang Kuei went off to Nanking, the new capital of the National Government, to work in the office of the Secretary of the Central Executive Committee of the Kuomintang, as an editor of the *Central Party Affairs Monthly.*

Sometime in 1928 or 1929, Chiang Kuei paid a visit to Tsinan. There he sought out the singing-girl Chin-tzu, with whom he had been in love at the age of fifteen. Although they had been separated for four or five years, they found that their feelings remained much the same. Although Chin-tzu's elder sister had married and Chin-tzu was now the sole support of her mother, the mother declared that she still would welcome her daughter's match with Chiang Kuei. Chin-tzu's profession was not considered a very respectable one and marriage to a young man of Chiang Kuei's family status was much to be desired.

Chiang Kuei could not make up his mind between the Tsinan singing-girl and the Shanghai nurse. At length, he told Chin-tzu that he needed more time to think and returned to Nanking. After a few months of deliberation, he went to Shanghai and married Yen Hsüeh-mei in May 1929.

After the marriage, Yen Hsüeh-mei went to Chen-chiang to work in the Kiangsu Provincial Hospital and Chiang Kuei returned to his job in Nanking. But he had not seen the last of Chin-tzu. Before long, she and her mother arrived in Nanking. Chin-tzu sang at the *Ch'ing-ch'ang kuan* (Quiet Singing Hall) near the Confucian Temple in Nanking, and one day, passing by, he noticed her name in gold characters on a red billboard. He did not go in, but inevitably they met, and as old friends whose feelings for one another were still alive, they began to see each other covertly.

The secrecy seems to have been dictated by two considerations. One was that Chin-tzu's mother assumed that their relationship had ended when Chiang Kuei chose a different bride. The other was that Chin-tzu was now in her twenties and just past her youthful prime; her chances of attracting suitors might have been damaged if Chiang Kuei had been seen too much in her company.

Of course Chiang Kuei's wife found out about her husband's companion, although in an unusual way and with unusual results. The nurses at the hospital in Chen-chiang where Yen Hsüeh-mei worked often amused themselves putting questions to the Chinese equivalent of a Ouija board. One day the device informed Yen Hsüeh-mei that her husband was running around with a girl friend in Nanking. Yen Hsüeh-mei did not take the Ouija board seriously but all the same she made a surprise visit to Nanking and confronted Chiang Kuei. She announced that she had come to see his girl friend. Chiang Kuei, amazed, admitted that he had been seeing Chin-tzu but insisted that their relationship was innocent. Yen

Hsüeh-mei then demanded that he invite Chin-tzu to dinner. A week later, a dinner was arranged and the wife met the "sweetheart" face to face.

After that, the two young women became fast friends and saw each other frequently. Their friendship continued until Chin-tzu and her mother returned to the north. Chiang Kuei never saw Chin-tzu again. In memory of her, he resolved never again to enter a singing establishment and he kept his resolve.

It was probably in 1929 that Chiang Kuei moved to Shanghai and began to write. He lived with his wife at the Chüeh-lu (Wealth and Nobility) Hotel on Hsi-tsang (Tibet) Road in the International Settlement of Shanghai, near the racecourse on Nanking Road. It is not likely that he joined any of the literary camps described above, for he was young and only on the threshold of his own career as a writer. Judging by the character of his later novels, his own literary sympathies and convictions probably would have placed him closest to the Literary Research Society to which his uncle Wang T'ung-chao and Mao Tun belonged.

Chiang Kuei's first novel, *Hsi-tso* (Exercise), a romantic tragedy, was published in 1929 by Hung Hsüeh-fan's *Hsien-tai shu-chü* (Contemporary Bookstore) on Ssu-ma Road in Shanghai. The first edition of two thousand copies sold out, but when Chiang Kuei wished to revise it, the publisher had died and the bookstore had shut down. A second edition never appeared.

His second novel, *Pai-kuan* (White Coffin), was sent to Wang T'ung-chao and was printed serially in the newspaper *Tsing-tao min-pao* (Tsingtao People's Daily). It was to have been published in book form by the Nanking Bookstore but because of a dispute over the price, it never appeared. The plot of the novel concerned a young man and a young woman who were in love. The young woman became ill. One night the young man came to inquire after her and saw a white coffin being carried into her house. He left and did not come again. Some years later, when the girl had become an actress and it was too late for the courtship to be renewed, he learned that the coffin had been for her mother. He never sought a wife.

In 1931, Chiang Kuei wrote his third novel, *Hei-chih mien* (The Face of Blackness). This novel dealt with the events he had witnessed four years earlier in Wuhan at the time of the split between the Left Kuomintang government and the Chinese Communist Party. The title expressed Chiang Kuei's feeling that the Communist Party belonged to the category of things "the reverse of bright" and that it had no future in China. But after consideration, he felt dissatisfied with his technique and burned the manuscript of this novel. Perhaps it was too soon to write about the events of 1927 with the necessary detachment and perhaps to have written honestly about those events would have been dangerous. But his experiences in Wuhan were not forgotten and were to find expression thirty years later in the novel *Ch'ung-yang* (The Two Suns).

III   *On the Eve of War*

Later in the year 1931, Chiang Kuei went to Peking, where he enrolled in the *T'ieh-lu hsüeh-yüan* (Railroad Academy) and received training in railroad management. This led to his appointment after graduation to a post in Hsüchow in Kiangsu Province with the *Ching-p'u* (Tientsin-Pukow) Railroad Office. He arrived in Hsüchow in the spring of 1935. The railroad administration housed the employees of Chiang Kuei's section in a hotel in Hsüchow and he lived there during the period of his employment until he left to join the army in the latter part of 1937. His wife did not join him in Hsüchow; probably she remained in Shanghai. Such an extended separation of husband and wife was not unusual in China and did not indicate any estrangement. It was often dictated by economic considerations.

Although in peaceful times Chiang Kuei might have been content to pursue the career for which he had trained for four years, the increasingly desperate situation of China precluded any such adjustment. Before long, he felt himself trapped in an atmosphere of intolerable frustration.

Japan held north China in a progressively tightening grip. The unsatisfactory post-World War I disposition of the Shantung question by the great powers in Paris in 1919 had been resolved by Japan's withdrawal from Shantung in 1922. But within a decade, the situation between China and Japan was again tense. Japan's Kwantung (Manchurian) Army had occupied Manchuria and the puppet state of Manchukuo had declared its independence of China on March 1, 1932. On January 28, 1932, fighting had broken out in Shanghai between Japanese forces and the Chinese Nineteenth

Route Army, and it continued until Chinese withdrawal from the immediate area on March 3, 1932. In the north, after fighting between Chinese and Japanese forces south of the Great Wall, China agreed in the Tangku Truce of May 1933 to withdraw her forces from the disputed area and create a demilitarized zone. Japanese military pressure in the north led to the creation of the East Hopei Autonomous Council in November 1935. This puppet regime claimed jurisdiction over 10,000 square miles of north China.

The railroad men were aware of the dangerous situation. But the hotel in Hsüchow contained a gaming room and a wine bar and prostitutes frequented the place, so that the hotel was commonly full of noisy activity and hectic gaiety. There was ample opportunity for diversion but Chiang Kuei felt oppressed and fatigued. Declining the invitations of his fellow workers to drink with them and ignoring the prostitutes who knocked on his door from time to time, he shut himself up in his room and wrote. His fellow workers wondered what he was doing alone in his room but he never told them the truth. "If I had honestly told them I was writing a novel, that would have given them a great laugh; they would have laughed themselves to death."[9] Eventually one of the other employees thought of a reasonable explanation: "He's writing love letters to his wife."[10]

In the latter part of 1936, the novel *T'u-wei* (Breaking Free) was completed. It was the product of his intense frustration: frustration with China's inability to counter the Japanese aggression and frustration with his job.

At that time the Japanese warlords were advancing daily against China, and my own situation was one of intolerable oppression, so I wrote another novel, *Breaking Free*. I hoped that I could break out of the circle of my life, and that my country could also break out of the encirclement by the Japanese warlords.[11]

The novel deals with the adventures of seven members of the petty bourgeoisie and the agitation produced in their lives by rumors of war. It is set in early 1932 during the time of the fierce fighting around Shanghai between the Japanese and the Chinese Nineteenth Route Army. This was a time of national crisis for

China, but the novel is concerned with the smaller crises important only to those who suffer them.

Chiang Kuei sent the manuscript of *Breaking Free* to Mao Tun, the established novelist whom Chiang Kuei had met in Wuhan in 1927 when Mao Tun edited the *National Daily* there. Some correspondence followed between Chiang Kuei and Mao Tun, and the manuscript was left in Mao Tun's custody when Chiang Kuei escaped from the frustrations of Hsüchow by joining the army.

When Chiang Kuei joined the army, he changed his name from Wang I-chien to Wang Lin-tu, taking as his new personal name the name—Lin Tu—of the most thoughtful and positive character in the novel *Breaking Free*.

IV *The War Years*

China's eight year War of Resistance against Japan, which began on July 7, 1937, was an epic of national suffering and endurance. According to a history published by the Ministry of National Defense of the Republic of China, China suffered 3,237,916 military and 5,787,352 civilian casualties during the war. Chiang Kuei was a small part of this great war.

After joining the Chinese Army in the winter of 1937, Chiang Kuei served throughout the war (1937—1945) in the Honan-Hupei-Anhwei Border Region in the Fifth War Area. Initially Chiang Kuei was stationed at Huang-ch'uan in Honan Province. Huang-ch'uan was two cities divided by a river. A poet named Chang Jen-min had once written: "The Huang River like a belt winds around the two cities," but Chiang Kuei found that the poet was mistaken; in fact, the river's course was straight. In this city Chiang Kuei met the man who was to become his closest wartime friend. Tseng Shao-hua was a young man from the southern city of Huang-ch'uan, and having enlisted in the army, he was assigned as Chiang Kuei's orderly. Later he accompanied Chiang Kuei to a new post in the vicinity of Lao-ho-k'ou, the headquarters of the Fifth War Area in northern Hupei Province.

By the summer of 1939, the major campaigns of the early years of the war were over and the situation was relatively stable. The Japanese held the China coast and the major eastern Chinese cities. The Chinese government had withdrawn from Nanking to Wuhan and from Wuhan to its final wartime capital, the city of Chungking in Szechwan Province. The Japanese bombed Chungking at will and waged sporadic campaigns in central China; the Chinese dug in for a war with no end in sight.

Chiang Kuei was ordered to travel through the war zone as far as Jananese-held Nanking and to investigate relations between the Chinese military and the civilians along the way. He set out, accompanied only by his orderly Tseng Shao-hua. He had bought a sturdy gray horse from a friend but since neither Tseng nor the porter they hired along the way had a horse, Chiang Kuei seldom rode his mount and it was used mainly to carry baggage.

Although their route took them through territory controlled by the Japanese and by local Chinese puppet troops, Chiang Kuei and Tseng Shao-hua wore their Chinese Army uniforms the entire journey because that way they could be sure of receiving assistance and information from the Chinese military units through whose zones they traveled. Tips that a certain road was safe or that Japanese troops were operating in a certain area were invaluable.

Chiang Kuei's route ran from northern Hupei through southern Honan and Anhwei into Kiangsu Province. He crossed the ruined tracks of the Peking-Hankow and Huai-nan railroads and found that the rails of the latter line were nearly invisible beneath the tall stalks of kaoliang.

At length Chiang Kuei reached Chiang-p'u county across the Yangtze River from Nanking. There he met the head of the county government who was still loyal to the Chinese government in Chungking. This man's wife, mother, and family had just been kidnapped by the Japanese, and years later Chiang Kuei could still see clearly the man's troubled face.

Chiang Kuei's return route took him through Shou-hsien where he rested for two weeks. When he arrived at his original starting point near Lao-ho-k'ou, the journey had taken seven months.

In the spring of 1940, Chiang Kuei's wife tried to join him in northern Hupei. The journey was difficult and dangerous. Yen Hsüeh-mei traveled from Chungking to I-ch'ang on the Yangtze River, and Tseng Shao-hua came from Lao-ho-k'ou to meet her. But the Japanese cut the return route and I-ch'ang was under day-and-night bombardment, so Yen Hsüeh-mei went back to Chungking. Tseng Shao-hua described the scene he had witnessed at I-ch'ang. The river was deep and rapid and the pier was dangerous. People had to wade out in the current and board as best they could. The crowds were desperate and it was each one for himself. Tseng Shao-hua had taken Yen Hsüeh-mei on his back out to the boat which carried her safely back to Chungking. He had seen a mother, whose child had not gotten aboard when the boat set out upstream, leap into the water and drown.

In the autumn, another plan was made. Yen Hsüeh-mei was to take the steamboat downstream to Feng-chieh, where Tseng Shao-hua would meet her and escort her overland to Lao-ho-k'ou. This plan worked and husband and wife, after nearly ten years of separation, were reunited.

For Yen Hsüeh-mei, the Shanghai-bred nurse, life in northern Hupei must have represented a striking change. Lao-ho-k'ou was the headquarters of General Li Tsung-jen, commander of the Fifth War Area. General Li's dwelling, as described by the American journalist Agnes Smedley, was very plain, with mud walls papered over, a ceiling of unvarnished boards, and an earthen floor covered with straw matting. If the General lived in such humble quarters, it is safe to say that the quarters to which Chiang Kuei brought his wife were plainer yet. But physical privation was nearly universal and in many ways Lao-ho-k'ou was an interesting place to be. The Political Department of the Fifth War Area operated a Japanese language school there, with two hundred Chinese students in 1939. The classes were conducted by members of the Korean Volunteer unit and by Japanese prisoners of war who were sent to Lao-ho-k'ou for indoctrination. Lao-ho-k'ou was also the site of six industrial cooperatives which employed refugees in a variety of trades. Foreign influence was present in the Norwegian Mission Hospital and the Italian Catholic Church.

Chiang Kuei and Yen Hsüeh-mei lived in a quiet village a little over a mile from the town of Yün-hsien, some distance up the Han River from Lao-ho-k'ou. In 1941, in the twelfth year of their marriage, a son was born. He was named Wei-lien.

Chiang Kuei was not able to remain for long with his wife and new son. In the spring of 1941, he received orders to report to Chungking to attend the *Fu-hsing-kuan* (Restoration) Central Training Institute. For one month he received instruction in Political Administration. Then he was assigned to further training at the Eastern Szechwan Normal School, where the subject was

"Enemy Intelligence." It was while attending these training courses that Chiang Kuei saw the face from his past, one of the members of Wang Hsiang-ch'ien's Society for the Study of Marxist Theory in Tsinan, but they did not renew their acquaintance. Although the Kuomintang and the Communist Party were partners in the United Front, the partnership was uneasy. In January 1941, a unit of the Communist New Fourth Army, through whose Yangtze Valley zone of operations Chiang Kuei had walked in 1939, had been surrounded, attacked, and annihilated by National Government forces, and the state of civil war between the two parties was by no means forgotten.

After arriving in Chungking, Chiang Kuei took the first opportunity to leave the grounds of the *Fu-hsing-kuan* and visit the hospital on Wu-ku (Arsenal) Street where his wife had worked as a nurse for three years. The hospital building, when he saw it, was unremarkable, but his attention was caught by the World Book Store shop across the street. In the window he was surprised to see numerous copies of his novel *Breaking Free* prominently displayed. This was his first knowledge of what had become of the manuscript which he had left with Mao Tun five years before. He promptly bought twenty copies.

What were his thoughts as he gazed at his novel with its unfamiliar cover illustration of lean and angry men surging forward, torches aloft? As he read the editors' preface, did its patriotic lines, summoning the artist to enlist in the national struggle and grow through hardship, seem applicable to his own life?

Wang Jen-shu, using the pen name of Pa-jen, had written an afterword to *Breaking Free*. Writing in 1939, he explained that the manuscript had been sitting on his desk for more than two years because the original plans for publication had been delayed by the beginning of the war in 1937. Wang, noting that the manuscript was written on railroad office paper, praised the "ungovernable pressure to write" which he believed had driven Chiang Kuei. He admired the economy of writing and the realism with which the characters were portrayed. Moreover, Wang Jen-shu felt that *Breaking Free* offered an accurate portrait of a certain pre-war social type: the "drab people" of the petty-bourgeoisie who were preoccupied with their own misfortunes.

Still, the general pessimism of the novel, which was qualified only on the last page with Lin Tu's resolution, was not in keeping with the hortatory preface of the Great Era Literary Collection. Wang Jen-shu, concluding his essay, expressed the hope that the "drab people" would become "revolutionary stalwarts" and that the author would take a more vigorous part in the cultural war.

One minor flaw in the book must have caused Chiang Kuei amused irritation. He had written the novel under the pen name of Wang Hsing-yen. Wang, of course, was his own surname. The character "*hsing*" as a verb meant "to do" or "to perform" some task, and the character "*yen*" was the surname of his wife. Thus the meaning of the pen name was that he had written the book for his wife. But the publishers had frustrated this intention by adding the mountain radical above the character "*yen*" which changed its meaning to "cliff, precipice, or grotto" and rendered his private meaning incomprehensible.

After three months in Chungking, Chiang Kuei returned to his family in northern Hupei. He was responsible for political work in the army and presumably was attached to the Political Department of the Fifth War Area.

The war dragged on, draining the strength of the Kuomintang and the National Government, replenishing the strength of the Communist Party. Across the breadth of occupied China, Communists were organizing the peasants to resist the Japanese. In the process they involved them in politics as the Kuomintang had never done and painstakingly built bases of mass support. Chiang Kuei must have witnessed the early stages of this process during his walking tour of the Yangtze Valley in 1939.

For four years, China had fought almost alone. Then Japanese bombs over Pearl Harbor brought the United States into the war and the "China Incident" was merged in the world struggle. China, as an ally of the United States, gained a limited access to the materiel pouring from American factories and arsenals and became the object of a host of American observers. These observers, following earlier reporters such as Edgar Snow, Agnes Smedley, and Evans F. Carlson, learned by 1944 that China was a land of heartbreaking poverty and misery, that the Kuomintang ran an authoritarian regime tempered by sloth and corruption, and that the Chinese Communists were dedicated, vigorous, and efficient.

The working style and the lifestyle of the Communists in Yenan impressed most American observers far more than the clique-ridden government in Chungking. Although T. H. White wrote that the National Government armies bore the main burden of the Chinese war effort, the Communist guerrillas received most of the attention in foreign accounts of China's war.

In the end, China's contribution to the Pacific War was to stay in it. China had absorbed much of the military might of Japan for eight years but America defeated Japan. China was left to bind her wounds and hopefully to emerge as the great democratic power of postwar East Asia. Victory had come at last; the newsreel photographs showed Japanese generals in China handing over their long samurai swords in bundles to the Chinese authorities.

Victory did not bring peace to China. The Chinese Communist Party was willing to enter a coalition government but only on terms which would reflect the new political and military strength it had gained during the war. The Kuomintang, which dominated the National Government re-established in Nanking, would accept Communist political participation in the government only after the Communists had integrated their military forces into the national armies. Chiang Kai-shek's government had secured recognition in a treaty with the Soviet Union, it was the sole beneficiary of United States postwar assistance, and it possessed an apparently overwhelming military superiority. Confidently, with American aid, the National Government rushed to reclaim the territories occupied by Japan in north China and Manchuria.

When the war ended, Chiang Kuei was a colonel in the headquarters of General T'ang En-po, commander of the Third Front Army, who accepted the surrender of Japanese forces in the Shanghai-Nanking area. Chiang Kuei left the army in Shanghai and went to live with his family in the Pootung District, south of the bend of the Whangpoo River. For the next three years, he worked as a banker and commission agent.

By this time, Chiang Kuei had lost or given away all twenty copies of his novel *Breaking Free*. He sought out his old friend K'ung Ling-ching, who was then the editor of the magazine *Hsin wen-hsüeh* (New Literature), but K'ung had no copies to give him. Neither did the publisher have any. The novel was to remain lost until 1969, when a single copy was located in the Harvard-Yenching Library in Cambridge, Massachusetts.

Shanghai, a city of six million people, the hub of China's commercial life, and the major outpost of the Western presence, was one of the last cities to fall to the Communist armies. But long before the first Communist troops approached Shanghai, a spiraling postwar inflation had wrecked the city's economy. Increases in the cost of living of more than one hundred percent a month drove the population to desperation; the black market flourished and rice riots were common.

Meanwhile, the National Government was losing the civil war against the Communists. Chiang Kuei's native province of Shantung had been the scene of Communist military activity since the beginning of the war against Japan and was the scene of much fighting in the civil war. Chu-ch'eng and Kao-mi, the towns of his childhood, were recaptured by the National Government armies from the Communist People's Liberation Army (PLA) on September 1, 1947, but the government lost control of Chu-ch'eng again on October 23, and of Kao-mi on December 1. Tsinan fell to the Communists on September 24, 1948.

Chiang Kuei's parents died under the new Communist order in Chu-ch'eng. Some of the younger generation may have survived but only Chiang Kuei is known to have escaped the mainland.

In December 1948, Chiang Kuei left Shanghai for Taiwan. His wife felt that he should go alone, while she remained with their children in the Pootung District of Shanghai. She felt that the disorders of a Communist victory, which by then was obvious, could not be worse than the eight year war against Japan through which they had lived. But Chiang Kuei insisted and they accompanied him to Taiwan. Thus, at the age of forty, he joined the emigrants who fled the mainland for better or worse to a final refuge on the island of Taiwan.

CHAPTER 3

Living and Writing in Taiwan

THE island of Taiwan was reclaimed by the Ch'ing Dynasty from the heirs of the Ming loyalist Cheng Ch'eng-kung (Koxinga) in 1683. It remained a dependency of Fukien Province until 1887, when it became a province in its own right. After China's defeat by Japan in 1895, Taiwan and the nearby Pescadores Islands were ceded to Japan. The gentry of the island, in a brief and hopeless episode, proclaimed a Republic of Taiwan but it was snuffed out by the Japanese forces of occupation and Taiwan remained a Japanese possession until 1945.

Liberation from Japan meant rule by China. In the postwar years, while the Nanking government waged a losing civil war, the corruption and mismanagement so familiar on the mainland were visited upon Taiwan by her new masters. Plague and cholera, banished for years by the Japanese public health services, returned. Prices soared. The Taiwanese were looted systematically by the mainlander administration of Governor Chen Yi. Whatever goodwill the Taiwanese had for their mainland brethren was exhausted after two years. Chen Yi's misrule brought on a spontaneous insurrection by the exasperated Taiwanese in February 1947. The insurrection was suppressed ruthlessly by reinforcements from the mainland.

Conditions were alleviated somewhat under Chen Yi's successor, Wei Tao-ming, a former Chinese ambassador to the United States, who was appointed Governor of Taiwan in May 1947. But Governor Wei's tenure was brief. As the military situation on the Chinese mainland went from grave to hopeless, the National Government prepared to make Taiwan its last refuge. Wei Tao-ming was replaced by General Ch'en Ch'eng. Martial law, which Wei Tao-ming had lifted, was reimposed by Ch'en Ch'eng. In 1949 came the great influx of refugees from the mainland, nearly two million people, including members of the armed forces.

Chiang Kuei's emigration coincided with the dismissal of Wei Tao-ming and the appointment of Ch'en Ch'eng. Chiang Kuei settled in the city of Tainan on the western coast near the site of An-p'ing, the seventeenth-century headquarters first of the Dutch and then of Cheng Ch'eng-kung. He attempted to continue the career of commission agent which he had pursued in Shanghai but his business collapsed in 1949. His capital was lost, his creditors brought lawsuits, and he was forced to declare bankruptcy.

Long before the case was settled, his means of livelihood had "fallen out of sight," in his words. "This was my first taste of poverty," he wrote, "and the taste was no good; however, I haven't been able to get rid of it." His wife was ill, he had three children to support, and he was without resources. When he looked back on his life, it was "all like a dream." The most painful aspect of his situation was that which he shared with many who had fled to Taiwan: "Country ruined and family lost."[1] Thinking over what he had seen during the past thirty years, he decided that he knew what Communism was, and that he could take all of his experiences and put them into a story. Thus, in exile, poverty, and hardship, he conceived the novel, *The Whirlwind*, in which he sought to portray the social conditions which gave rise to Chinese Communism.

Chiang Kuei began to write *The Whirlwind* in September 1951. Every day for four months, without a single day's break, he arose at four in the morning and wrote for two or three hours. The novel was completed on January 6, 1952. His hopes for immediate publication were disappointed and the manuscript gathered dust beneath his bed until he published it at his own expense in October 1957. The favorable critical attention attracted by that edition made possible the commercial publication of *The Whirlwind* in June 1959.

In 1953, about a year after he completed the writing of *The Whirlwind*, Chiang Kuei's wife was stricken with apoplexy. Circulation was impaired and half of her body was paralyzed; she became a bedridden invalid.

Chiang Kuei found work that year as the caretaker of a Roman Catholic church in the East Gate section of Tainan. By this time he was a Roman Catholic himself. Although raised in a Buddhist household, he had converted to the Anglican faith as a young man, and his wife, at the time he met her, was also an Anglican. In

Taiwan, Chiang Kuei read a book, *From London to Rome,* by an Anglican pastor who had become a Roman Catholic priest. This book, and his own thinking, convinced him of the truth of Catholicism, and he entered that church, together with his family.

The fact that he was a Catholic did not mean any rapport with the foreign priest. On the contrary, Chiang Kuei found his employer an arrogant, demanding, niggardly, and unfair master, and the seven years which he spent as church caretaker trying in the extreme.

His job required him to be almost constantly on the premises of the church, which meant that he had no days off and was on call at any time. During the first two years of employment, he slept on the plank floor of the church's upper story; later the priest provided him with a tiny bamboo hut containing a bamboo bed. No cooking facilities were available. Chiang Kuei rented half of a nearby kitchen in which to prepare his meals until a few years later when his employer paid for a bamboo hut for cooking.

Outsiders considered "manager" of the church a good position but appearances were deceptive. Since he was the only person on the premises, his duties included the menial tasks of sweeping the floors and cleaning the toilets, as well as answering the gate. He was paid somewhat less than the very modest wages received by a primary school teacher.

His life was complicated by the fact that his wife was an invalid and he had children who needed some care. The church was distant from the house where the family lived but because the location was on the outskirts of the city, rents were comparatively low and he was able to rent a decent small room near the church for his wife.

Chiang Kuei's second son, Wei-tso, went north to Taipei to attend the Fu-hsing Operatic Training School. His eldest son, Wei-lien, attended the First Provincial Higher Middle School, and his youngest son, Wei-yüeh, attended Primary School. Wei-lien and Wei-yüeh would make their simple beds in the church at night; for several years this served as their home.

All of this—the demanding, poorly paid work, and the irregular living conditions—might have been endurable if Chiang Kuei's employer had been a sympathetic person but he found the priest entirely disagreeable. The priest disapproved of Chiang Kuei's writing and felt that the time spent writing was time stolen from his job. In fact, Chiang Kuei did most of his writing in the early morning hours. The fact that his sleeping quarters were very near a factory which began its noisy operations around three in the morning helped him to rise early.

The strength of the creative impulse is evident in the fact that, despite difficult working conditions and demanding family responsibilities, Chiang Kuei wrote his most pointed and powerful novel under such circumstances. He began to write *Ch'ung-yang* (The Two Suns) in September 1959, and it was completed within nineteen months.

Chiang Kuei's intense dislike of his working conditions and wages, his antipathy toward his employer, and his conviction that he was cheated and exploited, found expression in his writing. The foreign priest became the original for the hypocritical French arms merchant, M. Lefebvre, who employs and exploits the young Hung T'ung-yeh, in *The Two Suns*.

Chiang Kuei paid for the printing of three thousand copies, which he sold to the Tso-p'in Publishing Company of Taipei. *The Two Suns* was published in May 1961.

In the month following publication, Chiang Kuei decided to leave his job. He had worked for seven years under galling conditions and his employer's decision to increase his work load without increasing his wages caused him to feel that he could no longer bear the burden. He rented quarters and moved his family into them, and amidst the confusion of moving, his wife died at the end of June 1961.

Her death was certified originally as due to the protracted illness which had kept her bedridden for eight years, and the body was laid to rest. Quite unexpectedly, in August he was accused of having permitted his wife to starve to death through neglect. The medical determination of the court doctor that Chiang Kuei's wife had died as a result of her illness was disregarded. The fact that he was not with her at the time of her death was held against him.

Chiang Kuei had no lawyer during his trial or appeals because he could not afford one. However, he received legal advice from Wang Ching-yüan, an attorney, and later from another lawyer named Hu Yü-chieh. It was Hu Yü-chieh who remarked: "The husband is not guilty; having no money was guilty."

Chiang Kuei pondered this remark and later wrote of it:

But I've never, to this day, been able to penetrate to its hidden meaning. Perhaps it means if I had had the money to allow my wife to spend the rest of her life in a hospital, or to summon a specialist to take care of her, then I would not have been guilty?
Who told you to have no money?[2]

Fearing the worst, Chiang Kuei bought a bottle of sleeping pills and planned to take his own life if he were sentenced to a long prison term. In August 1961 he was sentenced to a term of three years and six months. As soon as his trial and sentence were made known, much sympathy and support were forthcoming. Pending the outcome of an appeal, he remained at liberty.

Dr. Hu Shih had been one of those to whom Chiang Kuei had sent a copy of the first edition of *The Whirlwind*. He had responded with a letter full of warm praise for the novel. In 1960, Chiang Kuei had attended commencement ceremonies at Ch'eng-kung University at which Dr. Hu Shih delivered an address. After the speech, Chiang Kuei introduced himself and recalled that he had heard him speak many years before at First Provincial Middle School in Tsinan. Dr. Hu Shih remembered the occasion and they exchanged a few words; that was the first and last time that Chiang Kuei spoke to Dr. Hu Shih. When Dr. Hu Shih learned of Chiang Kuei's conviction and pending prison sentence, he wrote him a letter of inquiry and concern. No doubt interest in his case from Dr. Hu Shih, as well as many other literary men, helped him to avoid serving a sentence. Later on, when Dr. Hu Shih was President of the Academia Sinica, he wrote inviting Chiang Kuei to visit him for a few days but Chiang Kuei was never able to accept the invitation.

While he awaited a decision on his appeal, Chiang Kuei was without means of livelihood. Three days after announcement of the sentence, he received a letter from the *Chung-yang jih-pao* (Central Daily News), the government newspaper, asking if he wished to contribute a serial novel for the paper on a patriotic theme. In order to avoid starvation for himself and his three children, Chiang Kuei agreed to write such a novel.

I toughened the skin of my head [the equivalent of "gritting one's teeth"—TAR] and wrote thirty thousand words; it was really so painful that I couldn't go on and couldn't write any more, so I decided to abandon it and not write it. In this manner eight months passed; before long we had eaten everything up; there was not even rice gruel to eat. I saw my children so hungry that their eyes were full of tears and I couldn't bear it.[3]

Chiang Kuei resumed writing the novel *Ch'un-ch'eng* (Spring City), which was published serially in the *Central Daily News* and appeared in book form in 1963. The novel was propaganda, stressing the harmonious unity between Taiwanese and mainlanders and the value of the Chinese version of the Protestant ethic. Chiang Kuei felt that it contained ninety percent the ideas of others and only ten percent his own ideas.

In addition to *Spring City*, Chiang Kuei wrote some ten short stories between August 1961 and September 1964. These were published in magazines in Taiwan and Hong Kong. They were later collected and published by the Wen-hsin Book Company in Tainan under the title *Liu-yüeh shuang* (Six Month Frost).

In April 1963 Chiang Kuei's appeal from the original court decision was heard and the sentence was reduced to six months. Further appeals were made—the case was heard five times in all—and at last, in 1964, the original conviction was reversed and the burden of uncertainty which he had borne for three years was lifted.

While awaiting the outcome of his appeal, Chiang Kuei was asked by the editor of the *Chung-hua jih-pao* (China Daily News) to write a novel for serial publication. The result was *Pi-hai ch'ing-t'ien yeh yeh hsin*. The title is a line of poetry, which literally reads: green sea, blue sky, night night heart. Professor C. T. Hsia has suggested the translation *The Green Sea and the Blue Sky: A Nocturne*. However, the novel is referred to in this study as *Swallow Tower*. The *Yen-tzu-lou*, or Swallow Tower, is an ancient building connected with an historical incident which exerts a powerful psychological influence over the heroine.

Serial publication was completed at the end of August 1963, and he was asked by Shen Ch'iu-ho of the Pai-ch'eng Book Store to revise the novel for book publication. But matters connected with his continuing legal ordeal prevented him from working on the manuscript until the spring of 1964, and even then he was not able to carry out as extensive a revision as he would have wished. The novel was published in July 1964 by the Great Wall Publishing Company in Kao-hsiung and distributed by the Pai-ch'eng

Book Store.

Chiang Kuei feels that this novel, which is far longer than any of his other works and which draws upon his experiences as a railway employee in Hsüchow between 1935 and 1937 and later on in the army, is his masterpiece. Its greatest shortcoming, according to its author, is its excessive wordiness; it would have been better pruned by a third.

In 1965 Chiang Kuei moved from Tainan to Taipei, the capital city in the north of the island. There he eked out a living as a scenarist for Central Motion Pictures Studio and also wrote a number of novels which he does not regard as part of his serious work. Unlike his serious novels—*Breaking Free, The Whirlwind, The Two Suns,* and *Swallow Tower*—which are set on the Chinese mainland, his pot-boilers are set in urban Taiwan.

A prospectus for a trilogy of novels which would deal with the whole of modern Chinese history was prepared by Chiang Kuei in 1967. Collectively entitled *Ting sheng ch'un-ch'iu* (Annals of a Prosperous Age), the title is taken from a series of Peking operas which describe the heroic feats of Wu Yuan and Chuan Chu. *"Ting sheng"* means roughly "the peak of prosperity" and *"ch'un-ch'iu"* (spring and autumn) refers to the annals of the ancient Chinese state of Lu during the Spring and Autumn Period (722–481 B.C.) of the Eastern Chou Dynasty. The title, of course, is to be understood in a satiric sense, since the period described—1905 to post-1949—has been anything but the "peak of prosperity" for China.

Chiang Kuei feels that writing this trilogy depends upon whether or not his economic situation allows him freedom from want. Meanwhile, he lives quietly in Taipei.

CHAPTER 4

Breaking Free

THE seven main characters of the novel *Breaking Free* are Yüan Chung-hsüan and his wife, Hou Chün-yü; Li En-yüan and his wife; and three young bachelors, Wang Chin-chih, Ch'u Ch'ing-shan, and Lin Tu. All of the men, as well as Hou Chün-yü, are clerical employees of the railroad administration in Nanking and work under the supervision of one Secretary Chuang.

Yüan Chung-hsüan is an honest, unassuming, and rather timid person. His wife, Hou Chün-yü, is an excitable and aggressive woman, far more ready than her husband to resent any slight. Li En-yüan and his wife are Protestant Christians. The three bachelors are a mixed lot. Ch'u Ch'ing-shan is a completely frivolous person, a boaster, a drinker, and one who takes pleasure in ridiculing others. He is mean and spiteful but too petty and cowardly to be really evil. Wang Chin-chih is an extraordinarily handsome but selfish and shallow young man whose main concern is his sexual life. Lin Tu, a serious young man with a streak of independence, is the only character whose concerns transcend his individual fortunes.

These people are members of the petty-bourgeoisie and are separated by social class, education, and their urban background from the majority of their countrymen. All of them are aware of their difference from the "people," but only Lin Tu is disturbed by their estrangement. Early in the novel, he explains his exasperation to his friend.

Just now our department head instructed us. In this autumn of crisis, he wants us especially to manifest a relaxed spirit, and the sole reason is so that we can set a standard for the people. Just then I received a great awakening: we're no longer part of the people, we're of another sort, above the people. —What would you call that? I haven't yet found a fitting title! Suppose I say "ruling class"; that's a bit like it, but I don't want such glory! I take my little bit of salary, and every day I sell eight hours of my time; I feel that's enough, and I never realized that I'd stupidly sold even my own position among the people and belonged to this "class" of "rulers."[1]

The seven characters learn that the National Government is being transferred to Loyang, a city in Honan Province formerly the capital of the Eastern Han Dynasty, and that the department for which they work is also moving to Loyang. Fearful about their jobs, they hastily set out for Loyang. Their privileged position in society is again illustrated by an incident aboard the train. They share a boxcar with a group of peasants. The peasants huddle in half of the boxcar, chilly and uncomfortable, while the Nanking party eat and drink in relative comfort in the other half. An arrogant ticket inspector boards the train and flaunts his authority over the timid and ignorant peasants as he forces a helpless old woman who has ridden past her station to get off the train, leaving her stranded. Lin Tu speaks up, criticizing the ticket inspector, and because they are at least his social equals, the Nanking travelers are able to outface him. But the passengers on the Loyang train remain divided by class and background. After the ticket inspector has departed:

> The travelers opposite them [the peasants] also relaxed with a sigh, and at once grew a little animated, muttering in low voices as they discussed it, but their faces showed no emotion; it was as though they were of a different world, and were speaking of the affairs of a different world.
> The train, bearing passengers of different worlds and bound for different destinations, drove on westward, braving the wind and snow.[2]

When they reach Loyang, the travelers find a shabby provincial town which shows few traces of its imperial glory. The local rustics insist upon addressing them as "Your Excellencies" and defer to them, up to a point. This point is reached when Lin Tu discovers that his landlady is binding the feet of her seven-year-old daughter. Disturbed by the child's nightly screams as the bindings are applied, Lin Tu tells the mother she must not inflict this ancient abuse upon her daughter. Although frightened, the mother stands her ground and insists that she must bind her daughter's feet so that in the future the girl will not have to endure the ridicule of men. Lin Tu, confronted with this evidence of his country's seeming inability to accomplish even a modest reform, goes out and walks aimlessly in the street, muttering, "We haven't done anything, we haven't done anything." When Lin Tu approaches his landlady's grown son, a policeman who might be presumed to be more enlightened, the man is equally dedicated to the old custom.

One day, the Nanking party pay a visit to the temple of Kuan Yü, the God of War, in the countryside. The land is afflicted by a severe drought. As they walk back to town through the parched fields, they see some peasants toiling to dig a deep well. They wonder why the peasants don't get together to buy a mechanical pump to bring water from the river. While they realize that the peasants may simply be too poor, they feel that the real reason is their conservatism. Walking back to Loyang, they pass over the Lo River bridge built by Chao K'uang-yin, founder of the Sung Dynasty. Lin Tu reflects that the age of heroes seems to be all in China's past.

A curious incident at the bridge demonstrates that it is not only the Honan peasants who are conservative. An automobile flying the Kuomintang party ensign and the national flag drives up to the bridge and several dignitaries in old-fashioned long gowns and riding jackets emerge. Soldiers form files; obviously some important ceremony is about to take place. The bemused visitors from Nanking watch the local dignitaries kneel and kowtow near the bridge. One of the local officials tells the Nanking party that recently a small golden snake was captured nearby, believed to contain the spirit of the local divinity known as the Fourth Great One, and the dignitaries are praying to it for rain. The more sophisticated visitors from Nanking are amazed at this spectacle of superstition and the Christian Li En-yüan horrifies their local informant by offering to kill the snake for them.

Although Chiang Kuei never belabors the point, the import of this incident and of others in the novel is clear enough. China's modernity is a thin veneer, below which lies the stubborn backwardness and superstition of the vast majority of the people. Even the relatively enlightened citizens from Nanking are not entirely free of traditional beliefs. When Li En-yüan's wife, saddened by the death of her newborn son who died on the trip and bedridden with a lingering illness, takes her life with an overdose of medicine, Yüan Chung-hsüan, Hou Chün-yü, and Ch'u Ch'ing-shan insist that paper money and other articles must be burned for the dead woman's spirit and that a Yin-yang adept must be sum-

moned to predict the day upon which the spirit will return to the
scene of her death. When Li En-yüan, as a Christian, refuses these
suggestions, the others hastily move out. Yet superstition and backwardness are not the main obstacles to
China's progress. More fundamental, the novel seems to suggest, is
the tendency of the Chinese to accept oppression from their social
superiors and inflict it upon their inferiors. Thus, the Loyang
policeman Chang Fu defers to the visitors from Nanking but is merciless in evicting a widow with six children from a house so that he
may rent it to Yüan Chung-hsüan. The ticket inspector abuses the
peasants simply because he has the power to do so but shrinks from
a confrontation with the travelers from Nanking. Finally, Secretary
Chuang, who has placed Lin Tu under an obligation by granting
him an advance on his salary, insists that Lin Tu carve a poem onto
a seal for him. Early in the novel, Lin Tu complains:

What an unreasonable thing position is! We're men all the same, today
we're under his authority, and have to endure his anger; tomorrow he's under our authority, and has to endure ours![3]

Seal cutting was a minor art with which Lin Tu passed his time
and he resents it when Secretary Chuang's request turns his pastime
into a job. He feels that he is demeaning himself.

Lin, holding two pieces of old t'ien-huang stone, walked slowly back, feeling rather upset. He felt that the two things seemed to weigh a thousand
catties, bearing down upon him until he was about to lose his wits. It made
him think of a famous gentleman who had seen, in the old palace in Peking,
the satin-covered toilet left by the Empress Dowager Tzu-hsi, and had
written a poem about it, in which he said that this toilet, when he smelled
it, had a sort of odor of iris and rhododendron. He thought: "If this is a sort
of slavishness, then I'm a proper slave indeed, now! Weren't the craftsmen
of old placed in the same class as the prostitutes and the actors, since they
were all to amuse their masters? Who'd have expected that I'd fall into such
a trap, just because I cut a few seals to relieve my own loneliness?"[4]

The time spent at Loyang in the company of his fellow
travelers—they all resided outside the city in a compound which
they christened the "Peach Flower Court" in reference to a famous
story by T'ao Ch'ien—is intensely frustrating for Lin Tu. His com-

panions are petty people who pass their time in squabbling and idle banter and the atmosphere is one of futility. The nation faces a crisis and Lin Tu is concerned, but he is uncertain what, if anything, an individual can do.

After the death of Li En-Yüan's wife, Lin Tu stands alone in the dark courtyard musing. The Nanking group is breaking up: Ch'u Ch'ing-shan, Wang Chin-chih, Yüan Chung-hsüan, and Hou Chün-yü have departed for Nanking. The interlude at the Peach Flower Court has come to an end and all of them, like the Li's old maid-servant who is bewailing the death of her mistress, will have to take new roads in life. It seems to Lin Tu that the men of the present are captives in the shadow of China's past. He recalls that he had once hit upon a good line for a poem but abandoned it on learning that the famous T'ang Dynasty poet Tu Fu had written a similar line. Is it worthwhile to try to do something? After all, he reflects, even Sun Wu-k'ung, the magical monkey king of Wu Ch'eng-en's novel *Hsi-yu-chi* (Record of a Journey to the West), was helpless at last when he couldn't leap out of Buddha's palm.

Then Lin Tu receives inspiration and is lifted from his depression.

Lin Tu returned to his room at once. He thought, although Sun Wu-k'ung couldn't avoid defeat, still he did void his urine on Lord Buddha's palm, and caused the great Lord Buddha some small irritation; wasn't that his achievement? The world can never be your very own world! Friends, we'll meet again!

So he took out those two pieces of stone belonging to Secretary Chuang. He said to himself:

"Since I can never make him wake up, I may as well play a joke!"

So he carved these ten characters:

"The evening sun is limitlessly good,

But it is drawing near twilight."

"Aren't those also lines from I-shan? How is it he didn't remember them?" [5]

With this remark, the novel ends. Given the character of Lin Tu as revealed in the novel—thoughtful, independent, and concerned for his country and its unhappy people—one may assume that he will "break free" of his trifling employment with Secretary Chuang's department and strive to do something worthwhile, no matter what the odds. Even a small achievement is better than nothing.

CHAPTER 5

The Whirlwind

I Context

*T*HE *Whirlwind* was written during a time of sterility in Chinese letters. As C. T. Hsia has suggested in his history of modern Chinese fiction, the years of war and civil war were not conducive to creative writing. The situation in post-1949 Taiwan was even less so, as Lucy Chen has written.

At that time, the government had little interest in literature, except in terms of security. A ban was placed on the original works and translations of all leftist writers, living and dead. The authorities were seeking to preserve the traditional virtues and to indoctrinate the population as thoroughly as possible against Communism.[1]

At the same time, certain Chinese writers who had emigrated to Taiwan sought to organize writers in an association so that they could play their parts in the national struggle. The writers who formed the *Chung-kuo wen-i hsieh-hui* (Chinese Literary Association) on May 4, 1950, in Taipei shared the Communist conviction that literature was something to be organized and that it had a goal beyond itself. They felt that literature should not be a vehicle for escape but rather a stimulus to patriotic endeavor.

The publication of members of the Chinese Literary Association included such big novels as Wang Lan's *Lan-yü-hei* (Blue and Black), which was first published in 1957 and by 1964 had gone through nineteen editions and sold upwards of 52,000 copies; it was Taiwan's all-time best seller. Ch'en Ch'i-ying, a writer and journalist who was active in the formation of the Chinese Literary Association, wrote two long novels, *Ti-ts'un-chuan* (Story of Reed Village) and *Hua-hsia pa-nien* (Eight Years of the Hua and Hsia

Families). Like Wang Lan's *Blue and Black*, these novels dealt with life on the mainland in the nineteen-thirties and forties. But most novels published during this period, if they dealt with politics at all, did so in a crudely melodramatic way.

At about the time that Chiang Kuei was writing *The Whirlwind*, a writer named Ch'eng T'ieh-wu published *Nü fei-kan* (The Girl Bandit Cadre), a work which the critic Ko Hsien-ning described as "lacking the form of new fiction, but possessing the beauty of China's traditional literature, and with great power to move."[2] Ch'eng T'ieh-wu followed this novel with *T'ieh-mu erh-nü* (Sons and Daughters of the Iron Curtain), *Pao feng-yü-chih-yeh* (Night of Violent Storm), and *Mao Tse-tung-ti ch'ing-ti* (Mao Tse-tung's Sworn Enemy), but none of these came up to the standard set by *The Girl Bandit Cadre*. Later other authors wrote the same sort of anti-Communist stories, with frequently lurid titles such as Su Ying's *Wo shih Mao Tse-tung-ti nü mi-shu* (I Was Mao Tse-tung's Girl Secretary) and Liu Hsin-huang's *Hsüeh-yin tsai hsüeh-ti-shang* (Bloody Prints on the Snowy Ground). T. A. Hsia has described the content of a typical example of this *"fan-kung pa-ku"* (anti-Communist eight-legged essay) as follows:

A beautiful Communist cadre falls in love with a handsome Nationalist secret agent, to whom she loses first her body and then her Communist soul. She is consequently arrested and tortured to death by the villain, her ugly Communist lover, while the hero, after a miraculous escape, safe in Taiwan, smokes a government-manufactured cigarette, which he praises as better than anything he could find on the mainland, and begins to tell his sad story.[3]

Not all fiction, of course, dealt with political themes. There were many romantic novels and, on a more popular level, plenty of *wu-hsia* (knight-errant) stories. But no one had really tried to analyze in fiction the reasons for the Communist victory on the mainland.

II *Publication*

Against this unpromising background—deprivation of access, except through memory, to most of the recent literary heritage, a siege atmosphere, and an attitude of extreme, but uncritical, anti-Communism—Chiang Kuei wrote *The Whirlwind*. His purpose, as mentioned above, was to explore and portray in fiction the social conditions which produced Chinese Communism. This purpose, he felt, would be best served by creating a microcosm which contained all the elements of modern Chinese experience important to his theme. Thus, all the action of *The Whirlwind* which is directly portrayed takes place either in the city of T. (Tsinan) or in the rural Shantung town of Fang Chen, and the Communist protagonists of the novel are "only a band of local Communists."

While the purpose of the novel was didactic, Chiang Kuei realized that his efforts would be wasted unless the novel could attract readers. So the novel must offer the reader diversion. "By utilizing his goal of diverting himself, I would attain my propagandistic goal."[4] Chiang Kuei felt that the modern novels produced in China since the literary reform in the 1920s did not have the appeal, and so did not achieve the high circulation, of the traditional novels. There were two reasons for this: first, the traditional novel used the syntax and literary style of pure Chinese literature and combined the refined with the common, and so was acceptable to the majority of readers; second, the development of the plot led the reader on and genuinely diverted him. Therefore, in order to appeal to as many readers as possible, Chiang Kuei used the techniques of the traditional novel.

Originally Chiang Kuei had had an arrangement with Lei Chen to publish the novel in Lei Chen's magazine *Tzu-yu Chung-kuo* (Free China). But by the time the novel was completed, the magazine no longer wanted it.

Chiang Kuei had felt, after completing the draft manuscript of *The Whirlwind*, that it would be a simple matter to find a publisher at once. That had been his experience on the mainland; the two-year delay in publication of *Breaking Free* had been caused by the war. But after taking the manuscript around to at least ten bookstores, magazines, and newspapers, all of which refused it, he began to feel as though he had given birth to a backward child. Several times he thought of burning the manuscript, as he had done with *The Face of Blackness* twenty years earlier, but he could not bear to destroy it. He put it in a chest under his bed and there it remained for the next five years.

As he approached the age of fifty, the age at which Confucius "knew the will of heaven," Chiang Kuei reflected upon his disappointing situation and lack of prospects. Wishing to do something positive instead of merely lamenting his misfortunes, he retrieved the manuscript of *The Whirlwind* from its resting place. *The Whirlwind* had been his first choice for the title but he decided to change it because he happened to see a book with a similar title on his bookshelf. The title under which the first privately printed edition of the novel appeared was *Chin t'ao-wu chuan*. This title meant *The Tale of the Modern T'ao-wu*, or, as C. T. Hsia has suggested, *A Modern Leviathan*. The *t'ao-wu* is a beast of Chinese legend but the relevance of this title to the content and purpose of the novel lies in the fact that *t'ao-wu* was also the title of a history of the ancient Chinese state of Ch'u, a history written "to record evils in order to warn."

The author said as much in the last paragraph of his introduction to *Chin T'ao-wu chuan:* "I wrote this only with the purpose of 'recording evils in order to warn.'" He considered entitling the novel simply *T'ao-wu*, or *Chin t'ao-wu*, but on second thought rejected these as too old-fashioned and refined. At first he wished to use a reproduction of Michelangelo's *Last Judgment* on the cover of the book. This inspiration from Western religious art was not as alien as it may sound, for the author was a Roman Catholic at the time of publication. But a suitable reproduction could not be found so the novel appeared in a binding of simple floral design.

Chiang Kuei paid for the printing of five hundred copies of *Chin t'ao-wu chuan* by Ch'un-yü lou Printers in Tainan in October 1957. Some two hundred were sent off by the author to various eminent individuals in the world of literature. A few score letters were received in return as the book began to attract favorable attention. Two years later in 1959, with the recommendation of Mr. Wu Lu-ch'in (Lucian Wu), Chiang Kuei received the assistance of the United States Information Service office in Taipei and found a publisher for the commercial edition of the novel. The original title of *The Whirlwind* was restored on the advice of some of those who had read the novel and felt that *Chin t'ao-wu chuan* was somewhat recondite. It was published in June 1959 by the *Ming-hua shu-chü* (Ming-hua Book Store) in Taipei. The novel contained forty chapters and was five hundred nineteen pages in length.

III   *The Novel*

The Whirlwind is a fictional study of the decline and fall of China's old order, represented by the Fang clan of Fang Chen in rural Shantung Province, and of the simultaneous rise of Chinese Communism in the same area.

The central character of the novel is Fang Hsiang-ch'ien, an intellectual who belongs to the middle generation of the Fang clan and to the first generation of Chinese Communists. He is a transitional figure: at once a product of the old order and its dedicated enemy.

The first six chapters of the novel are set in the city of T. (Tsinan, the capital of Shantung Province) in the early nineteen-twenties. Fang Hsiang-ch'ien, an educated man in his forties, is employed as a Correspondence Secretary at a law school, but his real efforts are spent nurturing the tiny Society for the Study of Marxist Theory which he has organized. Besides Fang Hsiang-ch'ien, his daughter Fang Ch'i-hui, and his nephew Fang T'ien-ai, the Society includes the Middle School students Tung Yin-ming and Yin Chin-mei, and two young printers, the brothers Wang Ta-ch'üan and Wang Erh-ch'üan. They meet covertly and discuss Marxism and the Russian revolution, but their understanding of both topics is extremely sketchy. They are aware that Russia has had a great revolution, which they believe has created a utopian society, and they believe that China must follow the Russian path. This is about as far as their knowledge goes.

But if Fang Hsiang-ch'ien's theoretical knowledge leaves much to be desired, his dedication and certainty is complete and he is conscious of his pioneering role.

I am a sower of seeds, I am one who lays foundations. There will dawn a day when China's communist society has been realized, and people will come to know that my—Fang Hsiang-ch'ien's—blood and sweat were in it. Then this life of mine won't be counted an empty one.[5]

Fang Hsiang-ch'ien, in an interview with the president of the law school, rejects an opportunity to seek a lucrative official appointment which he might have gained by appealing to an old classmate who is now Premier. The rejection is easy for him because he is certain that the old society is doomed. As he tells the president:

China's problem is not one that can be resolved by changing
Premiers. . . . Already the May Fourth Movement has made a cultural
revolution; everyone is aware of this. A cultural revolution is often the
beginning of a social revolution. I feel that before long fiery changes will
take place in China's political, economic, and social life.[6]

If Fang Hsiang-ch'ien does not covet position in the old society,
neither is he jealous of his position of local leadership in the
revolutionary movement. Feeling that the progress of his group is
too slow, he sends to Communist Party headquarters in Shanghai
for a more experienced leader.

Shanghai sends a young "Bolshevik" named Shih Shen-chih to T.
in response to the plea and Fang Hsiang-ch'ien readily yields the
leadership to the new arrival. Shih Shen-chih, who may be a purely
fictional character unlike the other members of the group who
represent real people, is a man of a very different cut than Fang
Hsiang-ch'ien. Vain and cocksure, he dresses like a young official of
wealth and is soon involved in an expensive love affair with a local
opera singer. In his Party work, he stresses that the end justifies any
means. Where Fang Hsiang-ch'ien had sought to borrow money for
Party expenses from his cousin Fang T'ung-san and had even
pawned his beloved fur-trimmed coat, Shih Shen-chih prompts the
student Tung Yin-ming to steal his mother's jewelry and urges Fang
Hsiang-ch'ien to extort money from Fang T'ung-san by threatening
him with Communist reprisals if he does not pay.

"Hsiang-ch'ien," he said, "your manner is that of a patrician, of a typical
petty bourgeois, and it's fundamentally wrong. You must know that for us
the end justifies the means."[7]

Shih Shen-chih's machinations are successful. Tung Yin-ming
steals his mother's diamond ring and Fang T'ung-san contributes
some money. But there is a price to be paid. The Tung family's old
maidservant, accused of the theft of the diamond ring, takes her
own life. Tung Yin-ming suffers pangs of conscience on the
maidservant's account and is rebuked by Shih Shen-chih for this
petty-bourgeois failing.

Shih Shen-chih himself, however, is also subject to petty-
bourgeois failings. In an effort to support his affair with the opera

singer, he rashly attempts to extort money from Tung Yin-ming's father. Old Mr. Tung, a retired county magistrate, is more than a match for Shih Shen-chih. He sets a trap whereby Shih Shen-chih is arrested with a pistol in his hand, apparently in the act of armed robbery. He is swiftly condemned and beheaded in the street.

Shih Shen-chih represented a false Bolshevik. But Chiang Kuei is not saying that all of the early Communists were vain poseurs. The student, Yin Chin-mei, is quite sincere. A poor youth, he is a completely dedicated activist.

Yin Chin-mei's only shortcoming was that his body was not in very good shape; his usual color was bluish-white, and at times he coughed, as though he had tuberculosis. His friends urged him to go to the hospital for an examination, to see for certain if he was sick or not. He was never willing to accept this advice. His reasoning was:

"If I were examined, and they said I had tuberculosis, then what? Do I have what it takes for a long period of convalescence? Tuberculosis is a rich man's disease, it's not something for a poor boy to try. So I don't need to go see. I'm just an ignorant worker; the day that I wear out and die, then it's all over! That's all there is to a man's life!"

Analyzed closely, this Bolshevik Yin Chin-mei was an intense romantic. With the pessimism of the petty-bourgeoisie, he sought and provoked death, consumed his life, and doubtless took revolutionary self-sacrifice as other men take opium. In the early days of the Communist Party, there were many like him; Yin Chin-mei was only one example of the type.[8]

After the failure of the imported leadership represented by Shih Shen-chih, Fang Hsiang-ch'ien decides that henceforth he will rely upon his own leadership. He leaves his small Party group in T. in the hands of Yin Chin-mei and returns to his native place, the rural town of Fang Chen. He has resolved to leave off activities in the city and to create what he calls "Real Strength," an armed Communist organization in the countryside.

Fang Chen is the seat of the wealthy Fang clan, rural landowning gentry who have been established in the area for hundreds of years. Although their property is gradually declining, they are still the largest landlords in their county. Several separate households comprise the clan. The wealthiest household is Resting in Quietude Hall, dominated by the elderly matriarch, Old Mistress, the widow of an official. This household includes her son Fang Jan-wu, his wife Mrs. Fang, and their four children. Among the host of servants are Second Master Feng, the family steward, Chin-pao and Chin-hsi, two young manservants, and Han Ma, Mrs. Fang's personal maidservant. Finally, there is Miss Hsi-men, who was formerly the cherished concubine of Old Mistress's late husband.

Nourishing Virtue Hall, another household, is inhabited only by Miss Hsieh and Eighth Daughter Fang. Originally an ambitious young man married the epileptic daughter of a high official. The official provided his son-in-law with a concubine, Miss Hsieh, and it was Miss Hsieh who bore the man his eight children. The seven sons all grew up and left Fang Chen, becoming members of the Kuomintang and achieving important positions in the outside world. Eighth Daughter remained at home in the great hall. Although Miss Hsieh was her natural mother, Eighth Daughter treated Miss Hsieh as a left-over concubine and showed her none of the respect normally due to a mother.

The household of Eighth Mistress, whose husband Eighth Master had sacrificed his life in a local uprising during the 1911 Revolution, contained only Eighth Mistress and her son, Fang T'ien-ai.

The household of the Licentiate's Widow was more complex. The Licentiate—the last man of the Fang clan to achieve a degree under the old civil service examination system—had two children by his first wife: the boy Fang T'ien-hsin and the girl called Second Sister. By his second wife, the Licentiate's Widow, he had also had two children: the boy Fang T'ien-chih and the girl Fang Ch'i-ling.

Fang Hsiang-ch'ien's brother Fang Hsiu-ch'ien maintained his own household and had one son, Fang T'ien-mao.

Finally, Fang Hsiang-ch'ien's own household contained his wife, his son Fang T'ien-i, and his daughters Fang Ch'i-hui and Fang Ch'i-man.

Not all members of the Fang clan still resided in the ancestral town. Fang Hsiang-ch'ien's cousin, Fang T'ung-san, had sold his rural land and bought urban property. He resided in T. and led the life of a literary man of independent means. Fang Chin-ko, a wealthy and influential member of the gentry, lived in the county seat and returned only occasionally to Fang Chen. Fang Hui-nung, an elder member of the Kuomintang, resided elsewhere as well and never appears in person in the novel.

The Fang clan, seen through the eyes of Fang Hsiang-ch'ien and through the eyes of the author-narrator, represents a declining and doomed order of things. They live off their rents, but they have ceased to play any useful role of leadership in the area. Fang Jan-wu serves as the captain of the local militia, but devotes little attention to it and is not even aware of it when the Communists gain effective control of the militia company.

Most of the adult members of the clan lead lives of idle luxury and diversion. Fang Jan-wu is a reckless wastrel and indiscriminate lecher who is barely literate and squanders his property to buy the favors of prostitutes. Clearly in him the gentry tradition of literary culture and moral rectitude has run out. Fang Hsiu-ch'ien smokes opium and dabbles in traditional Chinese medicine. He is also a devoted student of various systems of Chinese divining and for-tunetelling. Old Mistress spends her hours smoking opium and tormenting her old rival, the helpless former concubine Miss Hsi-men. Eighth Daughter Fang has no vices except her habitual cruel-ty toward her natural mother, Miss Hsieh.

None of these members of the Fang clan are much aware of the state of their property; control in fact has passed into the hands of their stewards. Nor do they know much about what is happening in the world outside of Fang Chen except that the times are bad and getting worse.

Fang Hsiang-ch'ien, upon his return to Fang Chen, is able to see the evils of the old system clearly. When Second Sister, the step-daughter of the Licentiate's Widow, loses her mind because of the abuse she receives from her step-mother and takes her own life, Fang Hsiang-ch'ien considers the incident further proof of the bankruptcy of the old order.

Among them it was Fang Hsiang-ch'ien who shook his head the most; he felt the depth of this tragedy of an old-fashioned family, thinking that the relations between men could not but undergo a fundamental change, and this strengthened his revolutionary spirit.

"Since the time of the Taiping Rebellion," he thought, "we've ex-perienced everything, but to no effect! We only have the newest and the last road, and that is communism!"[9]

The madman in Lu Hsün's short story urged his readers to "Save

the children!" Fang Hsiang-ch'ien tries to win over the younger
generation of the Fang clan. In T. he had required his daughter
Fang Ch'i-hui and his nephew Fang T'ien-ai to attend the meetings
of the Society for the Study of Marxist Theory and he had sent Ch'i-
hui and another nephew, Fang T'ien-mao, to study for several years
in the Soviet Union. Back in Fang Chen, he establishes a private
night school ostensibly for supplementary education of children and
adults. The real purpose of the school is to put revolutionary ideas
into the minds of those students capable of accepting them. Those
who cannot are soon dismissed.

Fang Ch'i-ling, the daughter of the Licentiate's Widow, becomes
a student at the night school.

She joined in order to amuse herself. She had never attended primary
school, but at home, with her brothers, she had learned to recognize not a
few characters, and as to reading old fiction and reading songbooks there
was absolutely no question. Fang Hsiang-ch'ien would frequently develop
some strange discussions with the students. For instance: he has money,
why don't you have any money? Why can't you take his money and use it?
Or another instance: this big family, old and young, all rest on your back,
and they're heavy to carry, why not throw them down? Why are you still
willing to carry them?

These provocative questions were taken in not only by the poor and
wretched, but even the younger generation of the great Fang family found
them intensely interesting, and felt they were absolutely right. Such a one
was Ch'i-ling. One day her limited thinking was set free, and she slowly
moved toward the left. In response to Sixth Uncle Hsiang-ch'ien's
emotional summons, she, like Ch'i-man and T'ien-ai, finally became a
positive element.[10]

Winning over the young by an appeal to their sense of social
justice is not a hypocritical tactic on Fang Hsiang-ch'ien's part; he
truly believes in what he teaches them. Attracting the youth,
however, is only one part of Fang Hsiang-ch'ien's plan.
Simultaneously he sets out to create armed strength in the countryside. This is his "Real Strength" or "Greenwood" policy and it is
carried out with the assistance of his nephew Fang P'ei-lan.

Fang P'ei-lan, who is the second most important character in the
novel, is the only son of a famous local bravo who was unjustly done
to death by the corrupt local authorities. He swore to avenge

himself on the man responsible for his father's death. When the Kuomintang leader Chu Cheng raised a military force in Shantung Province to oppose President Yuan Shih-k'ai's attempt to make himself emperor in 1916, Fang P'ei-lan became a regimental commander. During his brief spell of authority before the regiment was disbanded, Fang P'ei-lan was able to catch and execute his enemy.

After the regiment was disbanded, Fang P'ei-lan might have become either a bandit chieftain or an officer in the local militia which the gentry maintained to protect themselves. But neither career appealed to him and he lived in poverty. His life was made miserable by the demands of his large family which he could neither feed nor clothe properly. He became a ne'er-do-well, a misogynist, and something of a nihilist. Beneath this unpromising exterior, Fang P'ei-lan was a man of talents, courageous, intelligent, generous to a fault, and possessing many contacts at all levels of local society.

When Fang Hsiang-ch'ien returns to Fang Chen, he cultivates Fang P'ei-lan and quickly wins him over to the Communist cause. The two men talk and Fang Hsiang-ch'ien explains that Fang P'ei-lan's poverty and suffering can be alleviated only by revolution.

"This kind of bitter suffering is not yours alone, in fact it is shared by great numbers of men. With this kind of social system and family system, man must have this kind of suffering. There's nothing to be done about it. If an individual wants to avoid this kind of suffering, it's not something that can be treated like a headache or a pain in one's foot. You need to have a thorough-going revolution against the present social system and family system, and then something can be done."

"We had a revolution in 1911. And in 1913, we had the Second Revolution, what was the use? It's still the same old way!" Fang P'ei-lan said, shaking his head.

"No, I wasn't speaking of that kind of revolution. That kind of revolution is a political revolution, or in other words, it's not a revolution at all, just a change of dynasties. I was speaking of a social revolution. A great revolution that will thoroughly destroy this old society root and branch and then, according to the ideal, build a new society from the beginning."[11]

Fang P'ei-lan wants to hear more.

So Fang Hsiang-ch'ien, in simple terms, told Fang P'ei-lan about the significance of the social revolution. Taking Russia as an example, he explained how Russia, since the October Revolution, was entirely like heaven. In fact Fang Hsiang-ch'ien knew nothing of conditions in Russia since the Revolution; he was merely glibly drawing a picture according to his own ideal.

"Since Russia went through the October Revolution," he said, "the social revolution has been accomplished. Everyone works, everyone tills the soil, everyone eats, everyone is equal, everyone has freedom. Freedom to marry and freedom to divorce. If your wife doesn't suit you, quickly divorce her, and get a new one. The state has established nurseries, as soon as a child is born, send him to the nursery, then you don't need to look after him, and you needn't have anything to do with him! If you're sick, the state has established hospitals to cure you free of charge. If you're old, the state has old folks' homes to care for you until you die. In general, people in Russia have it made!"[12]

Fang P'ei-lan is easily won over and joins the Communist Party. Naturally his understanding of Communism is even sketchier than that of his mentor, Fang Hsiang-ch'ien, but for him it is enough to believe in the necessity of a social revolution. With his extensive contacts on both sides of the law, it is not long before Fang Hsiang-ch'ien's "Greenwood Policy" is on the way to becoming a reality.

Fang Hsiang-ch'ien's work prospered after he had won over Fang P'ei-lan. The brethren of the greenwood [local bandits—TAR] for their own part had always felt that when the times were out of joint, it was the matter of a moment to sacrifice life and risk death. Now they had a goal, they struggled for the goal of a social revolution, they were heroic Bolsheviks.[13]

Having made a beginning, most of the efforts of Fang Hsiang-ch'ien's followers are devoted to raising Party funds and attracting more men. Funds are raised by robbery which is attributed to the ordinary bandits who infest the region in great numbers. After Fang Hsiang-ch'ien and Fang P'ei-lan have gained control of some of the local bandits, they seek to win over the local military forces. They are able to place some of their men in positions of leadership within the local militia. When a battalion of troops is stationed in a nearby hamlet, Fang Hsiang-ch'ien arranges a marriage between the battalion commander, K'ang Tzu-chien, and Fang Ch'i-ling, the daughter of the Licentiate's Widow. Since Fang Ch'i-ling has been won over to the Communist cause, she accepts—as a Party assignment—a marriage that otherwise would have been out of the question and weds the common army officer. She is able to win him over to Fang Hsiang-ch'ien's side, although K'ang Tzu-chien remains ignorant of Fang Hsiang-ch'ien's Communist identity.

While Fang Hsiang-ch'ien and Fang P'ei-lan pursue their purposeful course, other members of the Fang clan, who are more or less their contemporaries, drift aimlessly.

Fang T'ien-chih assumes the post of Correspondence Secretary vacated by Fang Hsiang-ch'ien. When he finds that he is being used by the Communist cell left behind by his uncle, he feels disillusioned with life and runs off to become a Buddhist monk in a monastery near Hangchow. The family fetches him back to secular life and finds him a job as president of the primary school in Fang Chen. Before long, Fang T'ien-chih seduces an adolescent student who becomes pregnant. Although his mother pays for the girl's abortion, Fang T-ien-chih has to resign his position. Later on, although married, he buys the girl as a concubine and shuts her up in his house.

Fang Jan-wu continues his pursuit of sensual indulgence. After one expensive prostitute imported from the county seat is bought off and dismissed, he sets his sights on Little Wild Girl, the local prostitute P'ang Chin-lien. To prevent her husband's liaison with this common whore, his wife procures for him an unspoiled country girl, the daughter of one of their tenants, as a concubine. But before long, he is again seeking to bring Little Wild Girl into his home.

These men are almost entirely unaware of politics. Fang T'ung-san, the literary gentleman, is aware of politics but prefers to stay clear of it. Here he is speaking to a young poet who also wishes to detach himself from politics, but is not sure that it is possible.

"Perhaps you know, ever since my youth I've never cared for politics. I've always felt it was not the kind of thing for people like us. Now that I see the conditions of struggle with my own eyes, I find politics still more oppressive. Someone said 'politics is a dark business' and I think he was not mistaken." ". . . From now on you can be indifferent to everything except being a poet, and not meddle in politics again."

"But can this be done, Mr. T'ung-san? As a contemporary man, can one separate himself from politics and stand alone? Can literature and art separate themselves from politics, and stand alone, and develop alone?"

"My answer to this question is, we can try hard to think of a way of divorcing ourselves from it, and by trying and trying, we can lessen our corruption a bit, and then a bit more."[14]

Chiang Kuei's attitude is that such an attempt is futile. The artist may wish to leave politics alone but politics will not leave him alone. At the end of the chapter in which the conversation cited above takes place, he adds:

They talked until very late, and it was still the same road. There was no place to which one could flee, like T'ao Yuan-ming's Peach Garden outside the world.[15]

The victory of the Kuomintang in its struggle with the Communist Party in 1927 and the completion of the Northern Expedition in 1928 deal a setback to Fang Hsiang-ch'ien's plans but do not ruin them. He shuts down his covert headquarters in a Taoist temple outside Fang Chen and instructs his armed band to lie low. The reaction against the Communist Party ruins his organization in T. and the defection of the brothers Wang Ta-ch'üan and Wang Erh-ch'üan shakes his faith in the revolutionary character of the proletariat because these men were the only genuine workers in his group. But he remains a Communist.

Shortly after the anti-Communist repression of 1927 and 1928, Fang Hsiang-ch'ien is sent by the Party to T. to assess the damage. There he encounters his nephew Fang T'ien-mao whom he had sent to the Soviet Union some years ago for study. Fang T'ien-mao's experiences in the Soviet Union have turned him against Communism. In a conversation with his uncle, Fang T'ien-mao attempts to explain why he turned himself in to the authorities as soon as he arrived back in China.

"Sixth Uncle, I was exhausted. Truly, I was exhausted past bearing, and I couldn't go on with that kind of life any longer. I need to rest." . . . "I was in Siberia, between the icy sky and the snowy ground, for ten years at one stretch. Each year had ten months of struggle with the bitter cold. In the winter I wore double layers of bearskin and still I couldn't get the best of that cruel cold. If you were inside, it was all right, but as soon as you went out the door, the wind blew and that cold breath struck right through to your flesh. In northern Manchuria, it was the same icy sky and snowy ground, and every day I was galloping along on horseback for upwards of twelve hours. I speak Russian words, I write Russian letters, I eat Russian food, I do Russian things, I even took a Russian wife, I've become ninety-nine percent Russian, and the only reason there remains one percent that hasn't changed is because I don't have Slavic blood. Sixth Uncle, the more a man is in that unbearable cold, the more he thinks of these mild springs and summers of ours. I used to imagine that lying barechested in the shade of a tree and fanning myself to enjoy the coolness, in that hundred and three degree heat, would be like being among the gods. I used to imagine that if I could speak Chinese words, write Chinese characters, eat Chinese food, do Chinese things, and return to a Chinese household, that it would be no less than being a god among gods. When I had been riding to the point of utter exhaustion, I used to imagine a soft couch. When I fired the Russian big guns, I always thought of the firecrackers in our house at New Year's. In such a mood, when the International sent me back, I didn't even have to think it over, I turned myself in as soon as I got to Shanghai. I was exhausted, I had to have a rest. I still remember, when I first got back, I couldn't even speak Chinese readily, I had to think slowly, and talk slowly, and concentrate like anything to find the right word, it wasn't nearly as easy as speaking Russian. As for Chinese characters, not only couldn't I write them, I couldn't even move the writing brush about. But I *do* like to speak Chinese and write Chinese characters. I don't know why, but I've always felt that this was the language I ought to speak, and the characters I ought to write. I can't take other people's things, I've got to do my own."[16]

When Fang Hsiang-ch'ien accuses his nephew of being unable to overcome his "bad petty-bourgeois stock," Fang T'ien-mao advances his own criticism, which is the clearest statement in the novel of Chiang Kuei's anti-Communist position.

"I don't think so, Sixth Uncle," Fang T'ien-mao frankly expressed his own view. "I feel that this is reality. The strength of reality is greater than anything. It's you, working with the Communist Party, who have departed from reality. What you're relying on is only a kind of ideal. It's just like those men who sought immortality by studying how to sit in meditation and fast, and would endure bitterness for an idea that could never be realized; there's truly no meaning in it."[17]

Fang Hsiang-ch'ien rejects this criticism. In a subsequent conversation with Fang T'ung-san and Fang T'ien-mao, he makes clear his opinion of Fang T'ung-san's opportunism and Fang T'ien-mao's choice of the Kuomintang government.

"Let me analyze the political attitudes of the three of us . . . First, as for me, I recognize that since the success of the Russian Revolution, a tide has been running, and China must certainly go the way of Russia. Because it is very clear that China cannot save herself by remaining foolishly passive while surrounded by imperialism. You, T'ung-san, you feel that there's no escape from the present political authority, and moreover you don't see what force might arise and succeed it, so you are willing to place yourself outside of politics, and see which way the wind is blowing before you'll say. And you, T'ien-mao, you feel that the present political authority will surely be able to manage, and can maintain its rule, so you run with it, and act as its hawk and hound!"[18]

Although somewhat chastened by the defection of his nephew T'ien-mao, on whom he had placed the highest hopes, and by the news that his daughter Ch'i-hui, who had also studied in the Soviet Union, has become a Trotskyite in Shanghai, Fang Hsiang-ch'ien remains dedicated to his vision of final Communist victory. He returns to Fang Chen and maintains his rural force in waiting.

The years between 1928 and 1937 figure little in the novel. A new county magistrate appears, clad in a Sun Yat-sen tunic instead of the traditional long gown and riding jacket, and riding in a mule-drawn cart instead of carried in a sedan chair. But like his predecessors in office, he is venal. In Fang Chen, the Communists make further gains and Fang P'ei-lan is appointed captain of the local militia. The Communists support themselves by banditry and by trafficking in the heroin supplied by the Japanese.

The outbreak of war in 1937 allows the Communists to gain control of Fang Chen. When the Japanese Army arrives in the vicinity, the county magistrate Ch'eng Shih abandons his post and flees; later he is captured and becomes a puppet county magistrate for the Japanese. In Fang Chen, a former bandit chieftain who has become a Communist sets up a rival county government endorsed both by the Japanese military and by the Chinese National Government's provincial government headquarters in the hills. The Communists form the Whirlwind Column out of their rural bands combined with the local militia. In secret collaboration with the Japanese military, they annihilate a group of guerrillas loyal to Chungking. The

Japanese occupation of Shantung Province, in fact, creates a political vacuum in which the Communists can operate with greater freedom than before.

Soon the Eighth Route Army arrives in the area and a regular Communist government is established in Fang Chen. The revolution for which Fang Hsiang-ch'ien and Fang P'ei-lan have struggled so long begins.

The traditional society of Fang Chen, represented by Resting in Quietude Hall, collapses without help from the Communists. Old Mistress over the years has bestowed a good deal of wealth upon the rascally servants Chin-pao and Chin-hsi who heated her opium. Fang Jan-wu has wasted most of the rest of the family's property upon prostitutes and the remainder has fallen into the hands of the family's corrupt steward. After Fang Jan-wu's death, the family learns that the money is all gone. The steward quits, the servants are dismissed, and Old Mistress and Mrs. Fang are left alone to face starvation. Thus, when the Communist revolution comes to Fang Chen, it merely completes the destruction of the gentry's way of life.

Since the purpose of the novel is to explain the Communist victory in China, how is the revolution in Fang Chen treated by Chiang Kuei? First of all, no attention is paid to any constructive achievements in the direction of social justice. Whether this represents the author's complete judgment of Communism is hard to say because considering the time and place of the novel's publication, he could hardly have said anything good about the Communists. Simply to portray them as human beings with disinterested, if mistaken, motives was a departure in itself.

The principal theme in Chiang Kuei's treatment of the Communist revolution in Fang Chen seems to be the reversal in the positions of the formerly great and respected and the formerly lowly and despised. The members of the Fang clan are among the first to fall. Old Mistress is arrested and the Provincial Committee Representative, the local Communist authority, demands that she make restitution for her family's ill-gotten gains as far back as the Ming Dynasty. Since she is destitute, this is impossible and she dies in prison. Eighth Daughter Fang and Fang Chin-ko are beaten to death at a public struggle meeting, and Eighth Mistress, the Licentiate's Widow, and her two sons, Fang T'ien-chih and Fang T'ien-hsin, also die at the hands of the Communists. When K'ang Tzu-chien attempts to protect his mother-in-law, the Licentiate's Widow, he and his wife Fang Ch'i-ling are arrested and executed.

But not all members of the Fang clan die. Some, by a combination of good luck and willingness to sacrifice any values left over from the old society, survive and even flourish.

After the Provincial Committee Representative has wiped out all of the local doctors and medicine shops in a campaign against the medical arts which he regards as a pastime of the bourgeoisie, he falls seriously ill and is saved by the uncertain medical skill of Fang Hsiu-ch'ien. He decides that Fang Hsiu-ch'ien is a "revolutionary doctor" and establishes him as chairman of the Revolutionary Medical Committee. The Communists particularly value Fang Hsiu-ch'ien's skill at performing abortions since this relieves them of concern about the results of their sexual indulgence.

P'ang Yüeh-mei and P'ang Chin-lien, the mother and daughter prostitutes of Fang Chen who had collaborated with Fang Hsiang-ch'ien and Fang P'ei-lan, have no ideology and act entirely out of self-interest. Because the Provincial Committee Representative falls in love with P'ang Yüeh-mei and comes to consider her "The Mother of the Revolution in Fang Chen," the two women achieve positions of great influence. P'ang Chin-lien becomes the Chairman of the Revolutionary Women's Committee. As such, she comes into contact with Mrs. Fang, the widow of Fang Jan-wu.

Mrs. Fang, once the wife of the richest man in the area, became a penniless widow after his death. She is saved from starvation because a Communist soldier, who had once been a poor mason in Fang Chen, decides to marry her. After this wedding of high and low, Mrs. Fang is obliged to become a maidservant to P'ang Chin-lien. Her docility and good manners win the favor of the prostitute. As a result, she is taken into the P'ang's establishment as a prostitute herself and before long finds herself bought for the night by a customer too shabby and repulsive for P'ang Chin-lien and P'ang Yüeh-mei. By the standards of the old society, she has reached the nadir of degradation.

Fang T'ien-ai, Fang Hsiang-ch'ien's nephew, returns to Fang Chen after the Communists have been in power there for some time. He has spent years of fruitless wanderings in southern China and returns home because he has nothing better to do. His mother has been put to death by the Communists, and from a friend who is now a Communist officer, Fang T'ien-ai learns the secret of success in the new order: one can choose self-respect or life but not both.

The choice is easy for Fang T'ien-ai. He learns that his uncle, Fang Hsiang-ch'ien, and Fang P'ei-lan are in disfavor with the Party. When the opportunity presents itself, he becomes the adopted son of the elderly prostitute P'ang Yüeh-mei, discards the once proud name of Fang, and becomes P'ang Hsiao-mei (P'ang who is filial to *mei*). He, too, violates the traditional codes in a decisive and shocking way.

By degrading themselves according to the standards of the old order, Mrs. Fang and Fang T'ien-ai achieve success and honor in the new. The Provincial Committee Representative eulogizes them.

"When all is said and done, in this entire district there are only two people who came from great families who truly confessed and regretted their crimes, who left that class without regrets, who leaped right into the great revolutionary furnace of the proletariat, who firmly grasped the revolutionary will of the proletariat, who became frontline fighters in the revolutionary movement of the proletariat: one is Mrs. Fang Jan-wu, who voluntarily married Old T'ao the Sixth, and the other is Fang T'ien-ai, who voluntarily recognized P'ang Yüeh-mei as his mother. Several thousand years of man-eating rites, several thousand years of moral obligations contrary to human nature, several thousand years of feudal virtue which killed people without seeing the blood, have been pitiably, and even quite laughably, crushed to bits under the brave actions of these two people. . . . These two people, a revolutionary beauty and a revolutionary hero, are worthy of the worship and emulation of all our revolutionary young men and women."[19]

The Provincial Committee Representative further shows his appreciation of the revolutionary conduct of the two by creating the Revolutionary Financial Administration Committee and naming Fang T'ien-ai its chairman. When the "Yellow Sea Bank" is established in Fang Chen, Fang T'ien-ai becomes its president and Mrs. Fang Jan-wu its vice-president. The two prostitutes, P'ang Yüeh-mei and P'ang Chin-lien, who have been guided all along by the principle of self-interest, also receive honor and deference.

It is only Fang Hsiang-ch'ien, the sincere and principled revolutionary, who is disturbed by the progress of the revolution in

Fang Chen. Initially he had been highly gratified to witness the culmination of his life's work. He willingly accepted the general poverty which the revolution brought to Fang Chen and acquiesced in the sudden execution of K'ang Tzu-chien and his wife. For a long time he tolerated what he felt was the arbitrary style of the Provincial Committee Representative. But when Fang T'ien-ai—who had been his own earliest protégé—is rewarded for becoming the adopted son of P'ang Yüeh-mei, Fang Hsiang-ch'ien can remain quiet no longer.

. . . . he felt that recognizing a mother and changing one's name was simply the senseless reactionary conduct of the bourgeoisie, left over from a feudal clan society. He said:

"Fang T'ien-ai was a Communist originally, but very early he turned his back on the Communist Party and entered the Kuomintang. Now he's left the Kuomintang and joined the Communist Party again. Such wavering conduct makes completely plain his insufficient resolve towards revolutionary knowledge and makes completely plain that he is a weak opportunistic counter-revolutionary element."

As for P'ang Yüeh-mei, so far no one had dared to have any contrary opinions about her. Now, Fang Hsiang-ch'ien publicly attacked her as well. He said:

"This old whore who won't die, what does she understand except smoking opium and white powder, making money, and enjoying herself with young men? She's completely a plaything of the landlord bourgeoisie and a reactionary element with the same interest as the landlord bourgeoisie. She and Fang T'ien-ai are just alike, secretly conspiring with the Kuomintang, spoiling the greatest possibilities of the proletarian revolutionary movement."[20]

Addressing the Forward Guard Unit of the Whirlwind Column in his capacity as their Political Officer, Fang Hsiang-ch'ien allows his emotions to get the best of him and says what is in his mind without discretion.

"Our proletarian revolutionary movement did not drop down from heaven. It was cultivated over many years, with countless lives, and countless blood and tears, so that we have the achievement of today. We cannot see this hard-won achievement ruined by the hands of a minority of running dogs of the bourgeoisie who feign to be revolutionaries."[21]

Fang P'ei-lan, alarmed at his outspokenness, cuts short Fang Hsiang-ch'ien's dangerous speech. Later, Fang Hsiang-ch'ien speaks of the revolution in terms a Confucian father might use in speaking of a wayward son.

"No, P'ei-lan, it's too pitiful to allow the revolution to be ruined by their hands! I made the Communist Party here single-handedly, it's like my own son, I can't see my son fall so low, I have a moral responsibility to teach my son. They've been so improper lately, they ought to beg my pardon as their elder!"[22].

The speech seals the death warrants of both men. For some time the Provincial Committee Representative and Hsü Ta-hai, formerly Fang P'ei-lan's leading retainer and now second-in-command of the Whirlwind Column which Fang P'ei-lan commands, have been looking for a way to remove the two elder revolutionaries. They are sent to the headquarters of the Provincial Committee in the hills, brought before a mass meeting, and condemned to death as counter-revolutionary landlords and agents of the Kuomintang. In a final violation of the filial code, Fang Hsiang-ch'ien's only son, Fang T'ien-i, secures his own position within the Party by denouncing his father.

On their way back to Fang Chen to face certain death, the two men are quartered overnight in a dank root cellar. At this point, Fang Hsiang-ch'ien realizes his mistake.

"I've been swindled by my own ideals. . . . Thirty years ago, I entered a long dream! Until today, when they've just helped me comprehend a truth. P'ei-lan, that which you and I have encountered is indeed like a whirlwind. I think, their ways being what they are, the future of the whole Communist Party will certainly be like that of a whirlwind. Although they rise all at once, in the end they must pass away in the twinkling of an eye, vanishing without trace or shadow, and becoming an historical example. Our personal situation now is very hard, of course, but from the viewpoint of the course of human evolution, the rise of the Communist Party is only an eddy which happens to rise within the tide. Going in the opposite direction, they will never have any possibility of reaching their goal, they have absolutely no reason to succeed. P'ei-lan, this is a truth."[23]

So the novel ends.

IV *Criticism*

T. A. Hsia has noted that book reviews are not a regular feature of magazines and newspapers in Taiwan. This perhaps accounts for the paucity of published comment, pro or con, on *The Whirlwind* and the lack of critical comment upon Chiang Kuei's subsequently published novels.

After the commercial publication of *The Whirlwind*, Chiang Kuei compiled a small volume entitled *Huai-hsiu-shu: Hsüan-feng p'ing-lün chi* (Sleeve Book: A Collection of Criticism on *The Whirlwind*). This book contains the introduction to *Chin t'ao-wu chuan*, the afterword from *The Whirlwind*, letters from Dr. Hu Shih and Chiang Meng-lin (Chiang Monlin), endorsements by three patriotic organizations, and eighteen critical essays by sixteen writers. With the exception of Professor C. T. Hsia's remarks on *The Whirlwind* in *A History of Modern Chinese Fiction 1917–1957*, *Sleeve Book* apparently contains the entire corpus of criticism on Chiang Kuei's works.

As mentioned above, Chiang Kuei sent out copies of his privately printed limited edition of *Chin t'ao-wu chuan* to various organizations and individuals in late 1957.

The Central Committee of the Kuomintang published an approving notice of the novel in the December 13, 1957, issue of their *Propaganda Weekly*, praising its style in conventional phrases and informing interested comrades where the novel could be purchased.

The Chinese Young Writers' Association published an endorsement of the novel in the November 1957 issue of their *Association Activities Bulletin*, which simply gave the names of the author and the novel, and the place of publication.

The Chinese Youth Anti-Communist National Salvation League General Headquarters sent the author a brief note acknowledging receipt of the novel and praising it.

This was the sum of official endorsement.

Dr. Chiang Monlin and Dr. Hu Shih each wrote to Chiang Kuei and their letters alike contained high praise for the novel's flowing *pai-hua* prose. Chiang Monlin went on to note the novel's fidelity to history.

The "Greenwood Policy" mentioned by Hou Ta [a Communist functionary in *The Whirlwind*—TAR] and the Kiangsi affair were completely the same, only the scope was different. This makes it clear that the means chosen in Kiangsi and in Fang Chen were the same. Local bandits, secret societies, Taoists, warlords, grasping officials, corrupt officials, local ruffians, dishonest gentry, local rebels, vagabonds, prostitutes, drug-traffickers, and a batch of ambitious intellectuals banded together to play out this "New *Shui-hu chuan*," thinking to "Take the place of heaven and carry out the Way." With Marx as the Heavenly Father, Stalin as the Heavenly Brother, and Mao Tse-tung as the Heavenly Emperor, they would carry out the "Way" of "Class Struggle."[24]

In the next paragraph, Chiang Monlin's analysis became more sophisticated as he noted the problem of the disparity between population and resources which had been evident and progressively more severe since the time of the Ch'ien Lung emperor (1736—1795).

Dr. Hu Shih remarked in particular on Fang T'ien-mao's criticism of his uncle's Communism.

There's nothing better than your use of *"hsiu-hsien"* (to seek to become an immortal) as a simile. Last year, in a lecture which I gave in Chicago, I also said: "The sort of society in which each does according to his ability and receives according to his needs is an ideal which has never been, and never can be, realized. So I paid particular attention to these words of Fang T'ien-mao. Those men who seek to become immortals by suffering for a forever unrealizable ideal—among them everyone calls on everyone else to suffer. Thus, the Communist Party, for an ideal that is forever unrealizable, slaughters human beings, and makes countless human beings suffer!"[25]

On the afternoon of June 13, 1958, Dr. Hu Shih, then President of The Academia Sinica, delivered an address entitled "Speaking of the Anti-Communist Movement from the Vantage Point of the History of Chinese Thought" at the National Political College. The burden of the address was a refutation of some foreigners who suggested that Chinese Communism was in keeping with certain aspects of the Chinese tradition and that the Confucian school had endorsed "equalization of the land" and dictatorship of the masses. Citing the thought of Confucius and Lao-tzu, Dr. Hu Shih maintained that the Confucian tradition was firmly grounded in ordinary human nature and that the morality of Confucius was similar to that of Christ. In fact, if the two traditions (Confucian and Christian) were to be compared, the Confucian was the closer to human nature.

Further on in his address, Dr. Hu Shih cited and quoted from the passage in *Chin t'ao-wu chuan* in which Fang T'ien-mao explains to Fang Hsiang-ch'ien that Communism is an illusory ideal which is forever incapable of realization. A *Central Daily News* reporter, knowing nothing of Chiang Kuei, and probably figuring that since he was unknown, he must be young, described him as "a young writer."

The eighteen critical essays by sixteen writers are repetitive if treated individually. Their contents can be summed up briefly.

All of the essayists praised *The Whirlwind* highly and particularly appreciated the author's mastery of *pai-hua*. Some commended the novel as an analysis of Communism and of the defects in Chinese society which allowed Communism to rise. As Kao Yang put it:

All those people who appeared during the time of *The Whirlwind* should have read *The Whirlwind*. One only feels regret that *The Whirlwind* appeared ten years too late. But when they were yellow leaves flying about in the whirlwind, how could they have known that they themselves were swirling in the current; this perhaps is the reason for *The Whirlwind* coming out late.[26]

It was most frequently compared to *Shui-hu chuan* and to *Dream of the Red Chamber*, and also, but less frequently, to *Travels of Lao Ts'an* and to *Ju-lin wai-shih* (The Scholars). These comparisons are valid only in a general way. The atmosphere of some of the episodes in *The Whirlwind*—particularly the story of the life and death of Fang P'ei-lan's father, Second-story Fang the Swordsman—is reminiscent of *Shui-hu chuan* and indeed Fang P'ei-lan is not much different from some of the heroes in that famous novel. The detailed family intrigues and the psychological analysis of character in the chapters of *The Whirlwind* immediately call to mind the *Dream of the Red Chamber*, the great Chinese "family" novel, but *The Whirlwind* is not a love story. Like *The Travels of Lao Ts'an* and *The Scholars*, *The Whirlwind* is episodic and digressive in the old style and its tone is satirical and pointed. These characteristics it shares with Chiang Kuei's other novels.

Perhaps the most interesting observation in any of these essays is found in Kao Yang's essay "On the Analysis of *The Whirlwind*." Kao Yang made by far the most intensive study of the novel and the essay is more than forty pages in length. Speaking of the history of Mrs. Fang Jan-wu, Kao Yang considers that authors have emotional feelings for their characters and that it must have taken exceptional fortitude on Chiang Kuei's part to put Mrs. Fang Jan-wu through these cruel changes. "Mrs. Fang Jan-wu," writes Kao, "in the Chinese society of thirty years ago, was a nearly perfect woman, who would have attained the love and respect of any man."[27]

Mrs. Fang Jan-wu is presented as an attractive character, sensible, determined, and capable of pity and disinterested benevolence; she also possesses a well-developed sense of self-preservation and self-interest. In an attempt to divert her husband's attention from the prostitute P'ang Chin-lien, Mrs. Fang Jan-wu attracted the virgin peasant girl Ts'ao Hsiao-ch'üan to her home as a servant. She conspired to drug the girl so that Fang Jan-wu could rape her. Ts'ao Hsiao-ch'üan was obliged then to become Fang Jan-wu's concubine. Later on, Mrs. Fang instigated her husband to murder the greedy manservant Chin-pao. At the end of *The Whirlwind*, what Kao Yang sees as her degradation is taken by the local Communist authority to manifest her whole-hearted identification with the new revolutionary values. She is rewarded with the most extravagant praise and given a position of responsibility and influence. What Chiang Kuei seems to be saying is that in the Communists' new revolutionary society, as in the old feudalistic society, shrewdness, adaptability, and the willingness to sacrifice self-respect in order to preserve life do pay off. Fidelity to long-held values and lack of adaptability, as in the case of K'ang Tzu-chien and Fang Hsiang-ch'ien, result in destruction.

The most cogent published criticism of *The Whirlwind* is found in Professor C. T. Hsia's essay on the novel. Hsia, who considers *The Whirlwind* "the latest flowering of the satiric tradition in China—from the classical novelists to Lao She, Chang T'ien-i, and Ch'ien Chung-shu" and "one of the greatest works of modern Chinese fiction,"[28] stresses the bankruptcy of Confucian values in the novel and the victory of anarchy.

Quite fairly, therefore, the author embodies in his heroes [Fang Hsiang-ch'ien and Fang P'ei-lan—TAR] the two strands of the Chinese tradition that are least decadent: Confucian intellectualism and the type of underworld chivalry *(hsia)* so celebrated in popular fiction. Yet even these two leaders are no bulwark against the forces of corruption inside and outside the Communist ranks. . . .[29]

In Hsia's view, the naïve utopianism of Fang Hsiang-ch'ien, who is acting out of disinterested motives but is willing to countenance wicked means, serves finally to liberate the baser impulses of lesser men. The result is anarchy.

The novel moves relentlessly toward anarchy. Yet the author is saying at the same time that Communism could not have come to power if the seeds of anarchy had not been already planted in the consciousness of the nonrevolutionary Chinese. Hence the ample space devoted to tracing the fortunes of the major Fang households—their unplanned self-destruction, in a way, serves an an ironic parallel to the systematic bringing about of social upheaval by the Communists. The sensualists, like the revolutionaries, are impatient with the human condition, and demand unlimited scope for their appetites.[30]

Hsia is correct in noting that the destruction of the gentry society of Fang Chen is self-wrought. His judgment on Fang Hsiang-ch'ien and Fang P'ei-lan, that "their quarrel with Chinese society is fundamentally an expression of disgust not so much toward the glaring national evils as toward the human condition itself,"[31] is questionable. While Fang P'ei-lan does exhibit a kind of nihilism before Fang Hsiang-ch'ien takes him in hand, Fang Hsiang-ch'ien is merely naïve about Communism. Fang Hsiang-ch'ien is not so much at war with the "human condition" as he is determined to replace a miserable and specific human condition with a brighter one. A Chinese Communist critic might point out that the very notion of a "human condition" common to all men is a bourgeois illusion which serves to obviate reforms.

CHAPTER 6

The Two Suns

I *Publication*

T HE Two Suns, which is a sister novel to *The Whirlwind*, dealt with the rise of Communism in urban settings: Shanghai and Wuhan in 1926 and 1927. As he had drawn upon the experiences of his youth in rural Hsiang-chou and Tsinan for *The Whirlwind*, in *The Two Suns* he drew upon his working experience in Tainan and his political experiences in Canton, Shanghai, and Wuhan in 1926 and 1927.

Chiang Kuei was aware that in writing of the events of 1926 and 1927, he was treading upon sensitive ground. *The Whirlwind* had attracted the suspicion of certain conservatives who felt that novels such as *The Whirlwind* and Eileen Chang's *Yang-ko* (The Rice-sprout Song) which, however anti-Communist they might be, treated Communists as human beings were propaganda for the Communist Party. In his introduction to *The Two Suns*, he included lengthy quotations from Chiang Kai-shek's *Soviet Russia in China* and stressed his own regard for Chiang Kai-shek as a far-sighted anti-Communist. For his own part, he wrote:

Historical fiction is indeed not history, and *The Two Suns*' story is completely imaginary. . . . My aim is only to re-create the singular atmosphere of that period, to give people a renewed impression, and a renewed understanding, as a "reminder of warning." . . . I have never believed that the Communist Party dropped down from heaven. We must dare to analyze those factors which produced it and later we can hope to extinguish it. Cursing and insulting can perhaps express our rage for a fleeting moment but in fact will not be of much use. It goes without saying that "concealing the disease and forgetting the doctor" is dangerous indeed.

To oppose Communism, one must be objective and one must be prudent.[1]

Chiang Kuei began to write *The Two Suns* in September 1959,
while at the church in Tainan. After completing the first eight
chapters, Chiang Kuei sent them to Fang Ch'i, a critic who had
seen one of the privately printed copies of *Chin t'ao-wu chuan* in
the winter of 1957 and had sought out the author in Tainan in the
summer of 1958 and talked with him. This first version of the novel
was entitled *Tu-hua chi* (Record of a Jealous Flower) and apparently differed from the final version, for Fang Ch'i mentions that a
woman appears in a prominent role at the novel's very beginning
and this is not true of *The Two Suns*. Later Chiang Kuei sent a draft
of the first chapters, some one hundred thousand characters in
length, to Lin Shih-ts'un, another friendly critic. By this time, the
original title had been changed to *Hsi-liu* (Western Currents).

In a letter to the critic Kao Yang, Chiang Kuei wrote:

The Northern Expedition was a turning point for the Chinese people from
weakness to strength. If the Kuomintang had been given cooperation and
allowed to carry it out, it could have turned out very well indeed. The
Communist Party, for the benefit of its own Party and in disregard of the
interest of the people of the nation, struck a blow [at the Kuomintang] and
caused it to develop a preference for the Right over the Left, to develop a
psychological manner of preferring corruption to evil, and thus influenced
its later defeat. It is only this *Western Currents* seeks to make clear.[2]

Chiang Kuei knew that the novel he was writing would be difficult for people to accept. As Kao Yang commented, "The period
after the May Fourth Movement and prior to the Northern Expedition was a vacant period of confused phenomena in a strange light;
contemporary people considered it fearful, and preferred not to talk
about it."[3] In spite of this, the novel was to be "even more bitter
and pointed" in its word portrait, and Chiang Kuei predicted to
Kao Yang that "this will be a painful business."

The novel under its final title *Chung-yang* (The Two Suns) was
printed in an edition of three thousand copies and published by
Tso-p'in Publishing Company of Taipei in May 1961.

II *The Novel*

The Two Suns opens in 1923 in Shanghai. The youthful
protagonist, Hung T'ung-yeh, has just graduated from Middle

School. He is the only son of Hung Pai-li, a revered martyr of the 1911 Revolution. His mother and his younger sister, Hung Chin-ling, have been working at the printing plant of the Shanghai Commercial Press so that Hung T'ung-yeh can complete his Middle School education. Although poor, the Hungs are an honorable and closely knit family striving together to maintain the good name of the martyred Hung Pai-li.

Hung T'ung-yeh's paternal uncle, a highly placed official in the railroad administration, refuses to employ his nephew, but finds him a place as an apprentice in the establishment of a Frenchman, M. Lefebvre, who operates a sporting rifle shop in the French Concession of Shanghai. Lured by the prospect of a bright future as a comprador, Hung T'ung-yeh labors for the Lefebvres for three years. He does the work of three men for miserable wages. Besides his routine duties, which include washing the underwear of his master and mistress and cleaning the toilets, Hung T'ung-yeh is required to study French in night school. By the time he has paid his tuition, bought his meals, and so forth, he is spending more than his wages and still has to rely upon his family for part of his support. In short, he is ruthlessly exploited by his employers.

M. Lefebvre is no honest businessman. His shop is merely a cover for importing weapons for the warlords and exporting opium. But his hypocrisy is surpassed by that of his wife. Chiang Kuei's sharpest scenes could scarcely be surpassed by any Communist author seeking to expose Western cultural imperialism. He points up the hypocrisy of Mme. Lefebvre and the abuse of Christianity in persuading the oppressed to bear injustice patiently.

One morning, as Hung T'ung-yeh was bending over to wax the floor, the Manager's daughter, holding a toy rifle, came running over and climbed onto his back, making him a horse, and telling him to gallop like a horse. This girl, although she was only eleven years old, was fat and probably weighed seventy or eighty pounds, and Hung T'ung-yeh was pressed so hard that he could barely draw breath. Hung T'ung-yeh knew that she was the darling of the Manager's wife, and going along with her, he crept a couple of paces forward.

"Good, I've learned to gallop like a horse, get off now."

She wasn't willing, and wanted him to go on, and the nine-year-old boy also got on. Little Sister sat on his back, and Little Brother sat on his behind, and they used the toy rifle to pound on his head, so that he would gallop faster. That pounding wasn't done lightly in fun, but forcefully and in earnest, and after a few blows, golden stars danced before Hung T'ung-yeh's eyes. He couldn't help being angry, and stood up violently, and the two children fell off onto their backs. Little Brother got up wailing loudly, and Little Sister took the toy rifle and beat wildly at Hung T'ung-yeh, hitting him on the head and face so that blood flowed in quite a few places.

The Manager's wife heard, and looked, and came running out; she pulled her son and daughter away, asked how it had started, and then blamed Hung T'ung-yeh.

"They're your little masters, and you're their horse, if they tell you to gallop, then you ought to gallop. You shouldn't throw them off your back!"

Having soothed the children, the Manager's wife brought from in the house a very thick book, and said to Hung T'ung-yeh:

"I've been wanting to say a few words to you for some time. It's very dangerous for a person like yourself to have no religion to believe in. You see that all of us in this household go to church every week, and are saying our prayers early and late. God dwells with our family. To serve your master and little masters loyally is like serving God, and God will like you. If God likes you, you'll be able to get along. If your master beats you, curses you, treats you like a horse, or a dog, you must bear it all, and you cannot have any spirit of resistance or dissatisfaction. Because God says, if someone beats you on your left cheek, you must also give him the right cheek. Let him beat you as much as he wishes, and never return a blow, even die without anger; that is God's will. Man cannot oppose God's will. After you die, God will invite you to go and enjoy yourself in heaven. Your uncle helps my husband to do business; they are friends, so I'm helping you to perfect yourself now, and telling you about this advantage. Oh, this is the Bible, you take it and read it, read at least one chapter every day; don't skip anything. This is in French, I don't know if you can read it well enough or not?"

The manager's wife, then, with her intimate expression, and her gentle tone, so sweet and honeyed, really seemed to be a different person than her usual self. Hung T'ung-yeh saw that this foreign Manager's wife was treating him with respect, and suddenly he was alarmed by this favor, and despite himself his body seemed to grow as light as that of a bird. He rubbed the blood off his face with his hand, and blushing, he accepted the Bible; he was so moved that he could not speak.

The Manager's wife went back inside, and seeing that the girl was still angry, she hugged her and said:

"You simply shouldn't get close to that yellow man! Naturally God will punish him, will send down calamities on him, just as he sent down calamities on the Egyptian Pharaoh."

Thus the sister and brother immediately knelt down before the bed, and muttered their prayers:

"God, God, send down calamities on that yellow man! Send him maggots, send him plague, send him blood! . . ."

God lived with them; they were soon happy again. From then on, they no longer paid any attention to Hung T'ung-yeh, nor looked at him straight on; however, at times they would call out in loud voices to him: "Yellow dog!"[4]

Mme. Lefebvre is accustomed, after her Saturday afternoon bath, to have a Chinese come and tend her feet while she relaxes with a magazine.

Taking a large picture magazine and holding it open with both hands to shield her from that yellow face, and giving him her feet, the Manager's wife knew a kind of complete and perfect happiness.[5]

When her regular pedicurist proves unsatisfactory, she requires Hung T'ung-yeh to learn the art and take his place. His erotic preference becomes permanently warped in favor of tall, buxom, white women.

After Hung T'ung-yeh has served the Lefebvres for three years at no increase in wages, his mother suffers an attack of appendicitis, and sixty dollars must be found for the operation. But when he approaches the Lefebvres for an advance on his salary, M. Lefebvre tells him that he must be joking, and Mme. Lefebvre tells him that they will pray for his mother; if it is God's will to take her, man must not hold her back.

However, financial help comes from an unexpected source. The labor union gives him ample money to pay for his mother's operation and convalescence. The source of the money is the young Communist from Hunan Province, Liu Shao-ch'iao. Liu is in charge of Party activities in the Chapei district of Shanghai and provides the money because he has seen Hung Chin-ling and wants to meet her.

Since Liu Shao-ch'iao is the most fully realized radical in Chiang Kuei's fictional world, it may be well to trace the life history with which the author supplied him.

Liu Shao-ch'iao is the son of a well-to-do merchant in western Hunan, a province noted for the volatility of its people. Originally his father operated a traditional cotton factory which provided clothes for the people in the neighboring counties, but economic and military factors beyond his control destroyed his livelihood. Foreign owned cotton mills in Wuhan, using modern methods, produced better material and sold it more cheaply and he was driven out of his own market. Mr. Liu, a progressive-minded man in business affairs, sent his third and favorite son, Shao-ch'iao, to attend the Textile Institute founded by Chang Chien in Nan-t'ung, and established a modern cotton mill in Hankow. There his Japanese competitors combined to exclude him from their market. He was driven to using various underhanded means, such as dancing girls, in his business dealings.

Warlordism complicated the problems of Chinese merchants like Mr. Liu. The local general summoned the Chinese merchants of Hankow to a banquet and informed them that since Peking had not paid his troops, they were on the verge of mutiny and would ravage Hankow. Thus the general found himself obliged to save the city by levying a contribution upon each merchant; when the sum demanded was paid, they could leave the banquet hall and go home. Foreign merchants and Chinese merchants under foreign protection were immune from such demands.

When Mr. Liu was ready to admit defeat and get out of the cotton business, he tried to sell his plant to the Japanese merchants of Hankow, only to learn that his machines were worthless second-hand Japanese models, painted and sold as new. He tried to make good his loss by a lawsuit in Japan but got nowhere. However, by selling his plant location in Hankow, he realized enough money to open a retail shop in the city.

Mr. Liu, although ready for the latest industrial techniques, still felt that parents should arrange the lives of their offspring. Having discovered a young woman of rare quality in Changsha, he overcame the reluctance of her elders with recklessly expensive gifts. In effect, Mr. Liu bought a bride for his son and thought that it was a match made in heaven.

But Liu Shao-ch'iao felt that his father had ignored his right to choose his own wife and he bitterly resented it. The marriage took place but Liu Shao-ch'iao insisted on treating it as nothing more than a commercial transaction. Contrary to custom, he demanded sexual relations with his bride on the wedding night, and crushed her resistance by remarking that, after all, she had been bought and paid for. Thereafter, he addressed her in public and private as "Fifteen Thousand," the sum his father had spent, and aside from visiting her chamber at night, he had nothing to do with her. Yeh P'in-hsia, the wife, who had been brought up as a model of the submissive feminine virtues, lacked her husband's spirit of resistance and endured the humiliating situation.

Liu Shao-ch'iao found a woman after his own heart in his wife's maidservant who had accompanied her mistress from Changsha to Hankow. Pai Ch'a-hua was a plump and merry young woman with a crippled leg and a stubborn will to self-assertion. Her former master, Yeh P'in-hsia's grandfather, had married her off to a crippled man with the cruel remark that since husband and wife were crippled alike, it was a match approved by both heaven and earth. Infuriated, Pai Ch'a-hua deliberately had made her unwanted husband miserable and neither beatings nor scoldings had bent her will. Liu Shao-ch'iao was moved to tears by the girl's story of resistance and individualism. He made love to her but refused to complete the sexual act, explaining that he was determined not to father a child. This was, he told the puzzled girl, because not to have children was the worst of the three ways of being unfilial; he meant to provide no grandchildren for his father.

When Liu Shao-ch'iao announced that he wanted to divorce his wife and marry her maid, his hunchbacked elder brother, who had hoped to marry Pai Ch'a-hua himself, was enraged: why should his brother have two women and he none? They began to fight, rolling about on the floor, until they were separated by their baffled father.

After sitting in melancholy silence for a while, Mr. Liu felt that he was without the strength to control his children; no words, no means could make them return to the right path. He simply did not understand their way of thought, and it seemed that they could not understand his way of thought. He thought, can it be that times are changing? Thirty years before, during his own youth, he thought that he had never had any difference of opinion with his father, or even with his grandfather; their ways of thought and their viewpoints were often the same.

What was the real reason that now there were great divisions between father and son, elder and younger brother, and husband and wife, and simply no hope of bringing them together?[6]

The response of Yeh P'in-hsia to the humiliation was to throw

herself into the river. She was rescued and sent to a hospital, and
Liu Shao-ch'iao and Pai Ch'a-hua discussed her case.

"It's a pity she didn't drown." [Liu said]
"You hate her so, it's too cruel. She's really a good person."
"I never said she was a bad person. I only hate the tradition and society
that she represents! Letting herself be cut up, willing to be a sacrifice, and
not resisting at all! Not to resist, but to sacrifice oneself—what can be
done? If she could be like me, that would be well."[7]

The incident was resolved between the Lius, the Yehs, and the
police magistrate. Yeh P'in-hsia would remain at the Liu house in
Hankow but she insisted that both Liu Shao-ch'iao and Pai Ch'a-
hua leave—Pai Ch'a-hua to the Yeh family in Changsha. Liu Shao-
ch'iao was tricked into believing that she would later escape and
join him and he went to resume his studies in Nan-t'ung. Pai Ch'a-
hua was beaten half to death and kept a prisoner. She was not
allowed to write to Liu Shao-ch'iao; when his letters to her went un-
answered, he believed that she had forgotten him.

Later Liu Shao-ch'iao transferred from Nan-t'ung to school in
Shanghai where he fell under the influence of radicals. He
neglected his studies and joined the Communist Party.

Liu Shao-ch'iao is able to gain an acquaintance with the Hungs.
His interest in Hung Chin-ling gets nowhere, but his influence
upon Hung T'ung-yeh is great. Liu Shao-ch'iao and his companion,
Ts'ai Wen-hsüeh, another Communist, live in rather bohemian
fashion in rooms above a hog-rendering plant which steeps the
whole area in revolting fumes. Hung T'ung-yeh becomes a frequent
visitor there. Liu Shao-ch'iao's individualism has developed into a
philosophical materialism which explains human behavior as
motivated solely by crude self-interest. He imparts this philosophy
to Hung T'ung-yeh.

"When your father and mother shared a bed and had a pillow in common,
did they have a blueprint to create a precious boy like you and sweat over
it? You just came along unexpectedly; the dregs of a necessary function,
that's all. People who eat food must wash the filthy and greasy bowl, and
you're the bowl. You must understand: in order to eat, they've got to force
themselves to wash the bowl, but they don't have to love the bowl!"[8]

Liu also contributes to the awakening of Hung T'ung-yeh's sexuality by giving him erotic books and by seducing him. Before long, Hung T'ung-yeh has to suffer the jealousy of Ts'ai Wen-hsüeh, who spitefully calls him: "Rabbit-boy" (the passive partner in a male homosexual relationship).

Finally, Liu helps Hung T'ung-yeh realize his oppression by the Lefebvres and urges him to rebel. Under Liu's guidance, Hung T'ung-yeh joins the Communist Party and thus comes under Party discipline.

Liu has explained to Hung T'ung-yeh his philosophy of leadership, which is much like that of the ancient Legalist Shang Yang: the art of leadership is the ability to dispense coveted rewards and dreaded punishments to one's underlings. When Hung T'ung-yeh is obedient, Liu rewards him by arranging an assignation with a European prostitute, and when he displeases, he is given a savage beating.

At the suggestion of Mme. Lefebvre, Hung T'ung-yeh supplements his meager wages by accompanying her to the northern beach resort of Pei-t'ai-ho and hiring out as a pedicurist to the foreign women there. An elder statesman of the Kuomintang, who knew his father, sees him there and urges him to give up such degrading work. This man puts Hung T'ung-yeh in touch with the Kuomintang agent in Shanghai, Ch'ien Pen-san, and soon Hung T'ung-yeh has become a member of the Kuomintang.

When Hung T'ung-yeh tells the Lefebvres that he is quitting, they immediately offer to promote him to assistant comprador and increase his salary tenfold. But he will have to perform his menial duties until another apprentice can be found and Mme. Lefebvre insists that he must continue to do her pedicure. To persuade him to remain, M. Lefebvre orders Chang the Comprador to take Hung T'ung-yeh out on the town for a night of debauchery. After a visit to a Japanese-run brothel, Chang and Old Wang, the Lefebvres' cook, try to convince the youth of the benefits of a comprador's lot.

"We all cluster around to eat from the foreigner's bowl; what have benevolence, righteousness, and virtue got to do with us?"[9]

Old Wang adds:

"Little Hung, forget about that business. Since you've been made Assistant Comprador, just muddle on with it and let it be. If you go to Ching Lung Lu [the street on which the local Kuomintang offices were located — TAR], wouldn't it be in order to serve? The taste of being a servant is much the same everywhere, it's better to remain where you are than to move."[10]

And Chang continues:

"No mistake, that's how it is. . . . When you put on the comprador's hat, there are certain advantages: you've got prestige, you've got food, and people are respectful toward you. When you go about with Chinese, your position in society all at once drops ten thousand feet, and who looks up to you then?"[11]

Despite these advantages, Hung T'ung-yeh decides to leave. The Northern Expedition is getting under way in the south, and when both Liu Shao-ch'iao and Ch'ien Pen-san are ordered to Wuhan by their respective parties, Hung T'ung-yeh decides to go south with Ch'ien Pen-san. When he does leave, Mme. Lefebvre lodges a false accusation of theft against him with the Concession police and he is taken to jail. Mme. Lefebvre visits him in jail to tell him the matter will be dropped if he consents to come back to work and attempts to give him a new prayer book. God, she says, will be with him even in jail; one cannot leave God.

Before his imprisonment, Hung T'ung-yeh had persuaded his younger sister Chin-ling to go to Wuhan with him.

"If I go to Hankow, I want very much to take you along."
"How about mother?"
"Mother is old, but young people are more important than old people. It's wrong for young people to be held back on account of old people."[12]

After his release from prison, Hung T'ung-yeh ponders whether or not he should visit his mother before leaving Shanghai. Chin-ling has departed with Ch'ien Pen-san, leaving old Mrs. Hung penniless and bedridden.

If I go, and see that she's sick and hungry, what can I do? Am I able to cure her, or feed her?

The answer naturally was that he was not.

Old people are close to death; they belong to the world that is past. We of the younger generation, however, have the responsibility of creating the future. Both sides should renounce each other and go quickly on.[13]

Hung T'ung-yeh abandons his mother and proceeds to Hankow where he becomes a liaison man between the Kuomintang, represented by Ch'ien Pen-san, and the Communist Party, represented by Liu Shao-ch'iao. In fact, he becomes a pawn as Ch'ien Pen-san and Liu Shao-ch'iao try to take advantage of one another.

Chiang Kuei, in his introduction to *The Two Suns*, claimed that Ch'ien Pen-san was not meant to represent the gentlemen of the Left Kuomintang, many of whom had repented of their mistakes and become orthodox party members of the Kuomintang. What Ch'ien Pen-san does represent is selfish opportunism, arrogance, and a blind refusal to recognize the destructive potential of the Communist Party.

Ch'ien Pen-san was a native of the district which produced General Wu P'ei-fu, and although he did not know the Jade General, he had friends in the Northern Army. As a young married man, he came to suspect his wife of carrying on an affair with the family cook and shot the man to death with a rifle, accidentally blinding his wife in one eye at the same time. It cost him a great deal of money to avoid the consequences of his anger and he learned the lesson that power came from position in society. He entered politics while still a young man and was elected to the Provincial Assembly. At the age of thirty, he was elected to the first National Assembly in Peking. "It was difficult," says the author, "to avoid becoming more or less corrupted in the official circles of Peking." Ch'ien Pen-san became more or less corrupt.

He was intelligent enough to see that the military strength of the northern warlords was ephemeral and must one day be replaced by something else. Having toured the Soviet Union during the famine, he was convinced that the Chinese people would never accept the sacrifices which such a revolution seemed to demand. When Dr. Sun Yat-sen assembled the Extraordinary National Assembly in

Canton to challenge the legitimacy of the Peking government,
Ch'ien Pen-san visited Canton and joined the Kuomintang.
Thereafter he managed a newspaper in north China and
propagated the ideas of Dr. Sun Yat-sen under the noses of the
warlords.

Ch'ien Pen-san was convinced that the Chinese Communist Party
had no future in China. But meanwhile, as a Kuomintang official,
he was willing to utilize the mass support which the Communists
had aroused to further the aims of his own party. Stalin is said to
have believed that the Kuomintang could be used by the Communist Party to the limit of its usefulness and then discarded like a
squeezed lemon, and this was Ch'ien Pen-san's attitude toward the
Chinese Communist Party.

In 1926, when the Northern Expedition was launched, Ch'ien
Pen-san was ordered to Hankow where his mission was to win over
Wu P'ei-fu's northern troops to the revolutionary cause. Through his
contacts in the northern military, he secured for his younger
brother, Ch'ien Pen-ssu, the post of a lieutenant colonel in Wu P'ei-
fu's Bandit-Suppression General Headquarters in Hankow. Then,
utilizing his brother's position, he was able to establish his own
secret headquarters in the relative safety of the British Concession.
He took an expensive room in the Hotel France in Hankow for his
residence, justifying the cost by the need for security in his secret
work. There he attempted to further the revolutionary cause by
obscure manipulations.

Ch'ien Pen-san wore an iron-gray satin-collared robe, sat in a deep, low
easy chair covered in white cotton, sucking at a large cigar. He had always
been accustomed to removing, replacing, and then removing again a pair of
big, thick, tortoise-shell dark glasses, which he wore during all seasons of the
year, early and late; this was done with his left hand. His right hand was
busied with that big cigar.[14]

In Shanghai, Ch'ien Pen-san had inducted the idealistic young
Hung T'ung-yeh into the Kuomintang. When he learned that Hung
T'ung-yeh was already a member of the Communist Party, he used
the youth to maintain liaison with the Communist Party and
ordered him to follow him to Hankow. Through Hung T'ung-yeh
he gained contact with Liu Shao-ch'iao, who was involved with the

Communist labor movement in Wuhan, and he tried to use the
Communist Party's influence to weaken the northern forces which
controlled the Wuhan cities. He dismissed any warnings about the
Communists that conflicted with his own opinion of them. When
Hung T'ung-yeh mentioned that the Communists claimed the
allegiance of seven hundred thousand organized peasants, Ch'ien
Pen-san derided the claim, saying that the innate conservatism and
localism of the peasants would preclude them selling their lives for
the Communist Party. His brother, Ch'ien Pen-ssu, took the Communists seriously and regarded them as potential enemies, but
Ch'ien Pen-san laughed at what he felt was his brother's obsession.

When the National Revolutionary Army arrived in September
1926 and captured Hankow and Hanyang, Ch'ien Pen-san
appeared in the open, proudly wearing a new Sun Yat-sen tunic of
fine quality and tailoring which he had had custom-made by a
foreign seamstress. He was momentarily embarrassed before his party superiors when his contacts in the besieged city of Wuchang
could not open the gates, but soon he was in his element as an official of the revolutionary government. While his new post on the
Government Committee proved to be meaningless, he nourished his
sense of importance by assuming command of the telegraph office,
where he busied himself checking all incoming and outgoing
messages.

Kuo Mo-jo, who was in charge of the Political Department in
Hankow at this time, must have been thinking of someone like
Ch'ien Pen-san when he wrote:

. . . at that time the majority of revolutionary comrades were fond of constantly stirring up this kind of silly fuss. They were three parts
revolutionaries, seven parts bureaucrats.[15]

Before long, the Left Kuomintang, supported by the Communist
Party, gained the ascendancy in Wuhan, and Ch'ien Pen-san readily
adapted to the mood of the day. At a mass rally, where the speakers
included Borodin and the Widow Chung (a character possibly in-
tended to represent Madame Sun Yat-sen), Ch'ien Pen-san praised
the Soviet Union and said that China must learn from the Soviet
Union.

Chiang Kuei pays relatively little attention to the historical events of the time and place. The vanity and stupidity of the northern warlords are detailed in a few episodes, the leaders Wang Ching-wei, Eugene Ch'en, and Borodin appear briefly off-stage, and the Workers' Pickets are a menacing presence from time to time. But Liu Shao-ch'iao's work among the proletariat of Wuhan is little mentioned although he is head of the Labor Union. Instead, Chiang Kuei concentrates upon the conflict of value systems and upon the mindless fanaticism produced by revolutionary passions.

The principal conflict of values in *The Two Suns* is between the Confucian value of filial piety (or, put in another way, concern for the immediate over the abstract) and an assumed responsibility for the "masses" (concern for the abstract over the immediate obligation). This conflict is not a new question for the author, for it appears in *Breaking Free*, written in 1936, when Lin Tu, who represents the author's point of view, brings up the matter of his friend Wang Chin-chih's mother. It is 1932 and fierce fighting is going on in Shanghai between the Japanese and the Chinese:

"Oh, isn't your mother in Shanghai?"

"She's in Shanghai. And she lives in Chapei!"

"Well, what do you plan to do?"

"What can I do?" Chin-chih heaved a deep sigh, saying: "she's eaten more than twenty years of bitterness on my behalf because my father died early; now I'm grown up, and she's still in the factory; as she got along before, so she's getting along now! I know that my having grown up hasn't brought her any good fortune; on the contrary it's added to her cares! A few years ago I felt deeply upset about this, but recently I've seen my way through. — What is the present period? Now it's a question of the masses. Unless the question of the masses is solved, the individual is out of luck, and this is my mother's fate. So I can't be narrowly concerned about her alone. I must be broadly concerned and follow the masses!"[16]

Since Wang Chin-chih is merely a clerk in the railroad office in Nanking and not in a position to do anything for the masses, Lin Tu's reply is sarcastic. Wang then defends his neglect of his mother by saying that he is unable to help her. Lin Tu, exasperated by his friend's disclaimer of responsibility toward his mother, responds:

"Indeed, I didn't say you ought to rush into Chapei and rescue her. Only

I think you're scarcely human."[17]

Later on, Lin Tu learns that Wang Chin-chih's mother lost her leg in the bombing in Shanghai and is living in an emergency hostel. Penniless, the old woman appeals to her son for help but he ignores her letter. In *The Two Suns*, the confrontation takes place when Hung Chin-ling accuses her brother of not caring for his own mother.

"She's old, she can't work."
"Then there's no way she can live." Hung T'ung-yeh shook his head and smiled bitterly. "In the future when the revolution is achieved, the nation will establish old folks' homes. Now is a period of change in which one year's harvest doesn't last until the next year and it's unavoidable that there will be many small tragedies."
"You call this a small tragedy?"
"Yes, we have even more proletarians who are suffering."
"If we can't even care for our own mother, how are we up to finding ways for the affairs of so many other people?"[18]

Hung T'ung-yeh seeks to excuse his neglect of his own mother by invoking his responsibility for the mothers of the suffering masses.

"How can you say I don't care for my mother? I'm opening a way for all the mothers under heaven!"
"Don't talk nonsense! When you don't even care if your own mother lives or dies, what could you care for other men's mothers?" Hung Chin-ling controlled her anger, and did not cry. "You see someone right in front of you dying and won't save her, and you say you're going to save someone 108,000 *li* away, you say you're going to save someone three thousand years from now—what kind of a heart have you got? Are you human?"[19]

In the context of this novel, Hung Chin-ling is stating the author's case against her brother and placing concern for the immediate need of another over concern for an abstract and distant goal. Her attitude may be called Confucian, since Confucius placed concern for parents above obedience to the state. Or it might be called Christian, since the author is a Christian. But simple humanity and natural filial affection is also an adequate explanation of Hung Chin-ling's attitude. She is not against progress or even revolution, but she feels that social responsibility begins with those for whom one is directly responsible.

Another debate takes place in the novel between Liu Shao-ch'iao, who advocates the complete destruction of the old society and all its moral codes, even the most basic taboos, and Hung T'ung-yeh, who draws the line at incest.

Liu Shao-ch'iao explains his quarrel with the old society: the favored minority live in ease and luxury by exploiting the miserable majority. The marital tradition, with its admonition of chaste widowhood, also has to fall. Liu argues that where a marriage exists only in the formal sense—as is the case with Ch'ien Pen-san and the wife he has abandoned—it should be dissolved. Even if the couple themselves wish to remain married, they should be forced to divorce since their minds are confused by tradition and if left to themselves they might not be able to break free: "Our first responsibility is to wake them up."[20]

Liu is determined to seduce Hung Chin-ling and demands that Hung T'ung-yeh help him carry out his design. He explains that he desires not the body of a woman but the destruction of an idea.

"I'm challenging a concept of virginal chastity. I want to destroy that selfish bourgeois concept of virginal chastity."[21]

Hung T'ung-yeh argues against Liu Shao-ch'iao's intention of forcible rape and writes a letter to a Communist agent in Shanghai to send his mother to Hankow, where he intends to use her as a means of controlling his sister.

While Hung T'ung-yeh wrote the letter, Liu Shao-ch'iao lit a cigarette and smoked. Pondering his theory, he suddenly came out with a strange notion, and struck his thigh hard with his right hand, saying:

"Challenge the old tradition, system, and concepts!"

Hung T'ung-yeh, seeing that he was very happy and seeking to please him, asked:

"Shouting slogans all by yourself?"

"It's no slogan," Liu Shao-ch'iao said excitedly, "Your mother's widowhood, which she is prepared to maintain to the end, is a concept of chastity. To sacrifice herself for the selfishness of the bourgeoisie—it's really not worth it!"

Hung T'ung-yeh's face burned and he did not reply.

"I'll make your sister and make your mother. We have a responsibility to make both become progressive persons!"

Liu Shao-ch'iao saw that Hung T'ung-yeh's face was wooden and that he did not answer and he said with a laugh:

"What, aren't you pleased? In order to attain the goal, in order to make them, anyone would do to 'charge the enemy and break through his lines,' it needn't necessarily be me, Liu Shao-ch'iao. There's someone who's ideal!"

Hung T'ung-yeh looked at him, obviously anxious.

"That's you!" Liu Shao-ch'iao stabbed his hand against Hung T'ung-yeh's forehead, saying: "You ought to do it yourself!"[22]

Hung T'ung-yeh pondered Liu's suggestion for some time.

"I can't accept your plan!"

"Your brain can't accept new concepts, isn't that so?"

"I can accept any new concept, but you can't order me to test it out on the body of my own little sister and on my own mother," Hung T'ung-yeh said painfully. "I can even say that if you ordered me to take a knife and kill them, I could consider doing it. Only, what you're hoping for, I can't do."

"I said before," Liu Shao-ch'iao said, shaking his head, "anyone would do for 'charging the enemy and breaking through his lines,' only it would be most fitting if it were you!"

"You also have a mother, how could you—"

"She died a long time ago. If she were still alive, it would hardly need you to suggest it, I'd have done it long ago."

"You're really a demon!" Hunt T'ung-yeh said with hatred.

"No mistake, I oppose God's laws and virtues!"[23]

Although Hung T'ung-yeh cannot bring himself to commit incest and is never called upon to murder his sister and mother, he does contrive toward Liu Shao-ch'iao's rape of both women. Before the split between the Kuomintang and the Communist Party drives him from Hankow, Liu Shao-ch'iao is able to strike a final blow against tradition. He arranges a marriage between widowed Mrs. Hung and divorced Ch'ien Pen-san; two traditions of marital fidelity are violated.

Elsewhere in *The Two Suns*, Chiang Kuei portrays, with some satiric exaggeration, the fanaticism which the revolution produces in its young followers.

Ch'ien Shou-yü, the daughter of Ch'ien Pen-san, is an intelligent and level-headed young woman. Her brother, Ch'ien Shou-tien, denied his father's affection, ran off to Kwangtung and joined the National Revolutionary Army. Wounded in the leg at the battle of Ting-ssu-ch'iao, he received poor medical treatment at a rear area station, and his condition is serious by the time Ch'ien Pen-san has him brought to a hospital in Hankow. Delirious and grinding his teeth in pain, the youth has become an automaton; he can mouth only revolutionary slogans:

"You've suffered!"

"It's nothing," Ch'ien Shou-tien ground his teeth, saying: "We revolutionaries must sacrifice!"

"I really respect your spirit!"

"We're walking forward on the bloody traces of the revolutionary martyrs, we must open the flower of revolution!" Ch'ien Shou-tien opened his eyes wide.

"You're really something!"

"We of the revolutionary party must knock down the warlords!"

Ch'ien Shou-yü saw that he kept grinding his teeth and batting his eyes and felt moved for him; she couldn't help asking:

"Doesn't your wound hurt?"

"How so?" Ch'ien Shou-tien shook his head, saying: "We revolutionary soldiers don't fear the pain of wounds."[24]

By the time he has recovered, the split between the Communists and the Kuomintang is apparent and he must choose sides. He chooses the Kuomintang and leaves Hankow for Nanking.

Chu Ling-fen is the daughter of the veteran revolutionary Chu Kuang-chi, head of the underground Kuomintang civil apparatus in Hankow. After the National Government is established in Wuhan, a personal feud between Chu Kuang-chi and Ch'ien Pen-san leads the latter to hint publicly that Chu is a counter-revolutionary and the Communists launch a campaign of denunciation against him. Chu Ling-fen is called before a meeting of her fellow students in Middle School. When she tries to defend her father, she is shouted down by the Chairman of the Women's Association who leaps onto the stage and leads the students in anti-Chu Kuang-chi slogans. Then the Chairman leads Chu Ling-fen away.

Two days later, Chu Ling-fen, pale and wooden-faced, appears
before another meeting and numbly denounces her father's crimes.
He has belonged to the Protect the Emperor Party and has caused
the death of revolutionaries; he has helped Yuan Shih-k'ai; he has
mismanaged the affairs of the school where he works; he has seduced as many as ten serving maids in one year. Prompted by the
Chairman of the Women's Association, the girl adds that her father
made incestuous advances toward her. Then the girl collapses and is
sent to the Common Benevolence Society Hospital to recover. Her
parents, summoned by the Japanese doctor, hurry to see her, but
she tells them to consider her as dead and no longer their daughter
and will say nothing more.

Chu Ling-fen does not hate the Chairman of the Women's
Association, who caused her humiliation and terror; she hates her
parents for being backward, reactionary, counter-revolutionary, and
feudal, and causing her all the trouble. Under pressure, she adopts
the point of view of her oppressors.

Her path is eased when she allows herself to be seduced by Hung
T'ung-yeh, who occupies a position of considerable authority as
head of the Workers' Pickets. With his aid, she enrolls in the
Women's Corps of the Central Military and Political Academy in
Wuchang and passes the entrance interview with Director Yen.

"Are you a virgin, or not?"
This question, coming suddenly as it did, caused Chu Ling-fen to have a
slight convulsion, and her heart leaped into her throat; she did not know
how to answer. Commander Yen understood, and said with a pleasant
voice:
"We're all women, and besides I'm your Commander, you are my student, and there are no strangers around, so just speak, and don't be anxious."
Still Chu Ling-fen was embarrassed, and she felt there was no way to
broach the subject, and Commander Yen was pressing her harder. Chu
Ling-fen saw nothing for it, she could only get up her courage, and
hesitantly said:
"I'm not!"
"You and who?"
Chu Ling-fen, ashamed, dropped her head.
"Don't be afraid, just go on and say," Commander Yen said softly and
warmly, "To whom did you give your virginity?"

"Hung T'ung-yeh," Chu Ling-fen spat out these three words towards the floor.

"Is that the Director of the Workers' Pickets?"

"Yes."

As soon as Commander Yen heard this, she was overjoyed, and ran over to grasp her hand hard, saying:

"Wonderful, you're not ashamed of a revolutionary progressive femininity. Because you gave your virginity to the proletariat, your body belongs to the proletariat. You're really thoroughgoing!"[25]

Chu Ling-fen is assigned to the unit led by Ch'ien Shou-yü, who befriends her. Shortly after Chu Ling-fen enters the barracks, a scene of political hysteria takes place.

A student was changing her clothes and was nude from the waist up. One beside her saw her and asked:

"Your breasts are so big, how is it that you don't wear a brassiere?"

"A brassiere?" The half-nude student responded with a question of her own: "How is it that you don't bind your feet?"

"Binding the feet is harmful to the body; that's not the same."

"Do you mean to say that wearing a brassiere is good for the body?"

When she was dressed, she rolled up her sleeves and said loudly:

"Brassieres are feudal and backward! I suggest that our corps ought to liberate itself from brassieres. One by one, let's open up for a look, starting with her!"

She pointed to the student who had just asked why she didn't wear a brassiere. Everyone, with a great shouting, all at once surrounded that student, and in a flurry of hands and feet, seized her, and tore into pieces the sleeveless waistcoat which had served her as a brassiere, and the student covered her face with her hands and cried.

"Dry off your tears!" another student ordered her.

"We revolutionaries shed sweat and blood, we don't shed tears!"

"Shedding tears is weakness!"

"It's like Lin Tai-yü! [the delicate, tearful heroine of The Dream of the Red Chamber—TAR]"

"It's like a concubine!"

"It's like a prostitute!"

"It's counter-revolutionary!"

"Down with counter-revolutionaries!"

When the unit leader, Ch'ien Shou-yü, intervenes to suggest a compromise, she becomes the object of attack.

"The unit leader is not revolutionary!"
She didn't know which student cried this out, but everyone began to bawl:
"The unit leader is not revolutionary!"
"The unit leader is counter-revolutionary!"
"Down with what is not revolutionary!"
"Down with what is counter-revolutionary!"
"Down with the unit leader!"
"Down with Ch'ien Shou-yü!"[26]

Chu Ling-fen does not want to join in the shouting attack against the young woman who has just befriended her so she stands silently to one side. But when another student seizes her and gives her a painful pinch and asks why she is not joining in the attack, she also begins to shout "Down with—." She knows that it is difficult to oppose the anger of the crowd.

Another writer might have employed a different setting—a workers' demonstration or a rural struggle meeting—to show politically inspired collective hysteria. It is typical of Chiang Kuei's satirical approach to set the scene as he does with a quarrel over brassieres, but the comedy does not disguise the frightening power of mass emotions.

The Whirlwind concluded on a note of qualified hope, but at the end of The Two Suns there is only foreboding. The unity of the Kuomintang revolution has been broken by the vanity and opportunism of the Left Kuomintang and by its refusal to see in the Communist Party a genuinely dangerous rival. Many of the youth have been lost to the Communists. The "good" revolutionaries, men who recognized the dangerous potential of the Communist Party, have been murdered. Chu Kuang-chi is killed by parties unknown and Ch'ien Pen-ssu is murdered by Liu Shao-ch'iao.

Hung T'ung-yeh was able to perceive the correctness of the Kuomintang's program of ridding China of imperialists and warlords. He realized that Liu Shao-ch'iao's program of breaking down the moral codes of traditional society would return man to a state of savagery, but nihilism made a powerful appeal to his emotions: he was able to wield power and gratify his sexual impulses. Not until the end of the novel does he break the psychological domination exerted over him by Liu Shao-ch'iao, and at that point, Liu Shao-ch'iao kills him. Liu's motive seems to have been personal as much as political; as Liu's final words to his victim—"It's your turn now, Rabbit-boy"—suggest, Liu despises Hung T'ung-yeh for his weakness.

As the novel ends, the Wuhan regime has collapsed. The Communists are in flight, and the party of Chairman Wang Ching-wei departs from Wuhan bound downriver. Aboard the steamer are Ch'ien Pen-san and his wife and daughter. Ch'ien Pen-san had foreseen the fall of the Wuhan regime in time to ingratiate himself with Wang Ching-wei, and he survives the debacle.

Liu Shao-ch'iao and his lover, Pai Ch'a-hua, also survive, to travel down the Yangtze. Thus, in the end, it is the scheming opportunist and the violent nihilist who live to shape the future.

III *Interpretation*

Chiang Kuei's approach to the changes wrought in Chinese life and thought by the New Culture Movement, the May Fourth Movement, and the Northern Expedition is ambiguous. On the one hand, he approves of the political goals of the Kuomintang: the expulsion of the imperialists and the destruction of the warlords. On the other hand, the uncritical rejection of the traditional moral codes and the collective passions necessarily aroused in the course of the revolution disturb him. Replacement of the code of filial piety by an untrammeled individualism or by loyalty to the abstract collectivity means the violation of natural human bonds connecting parents and children. In the atmosphere of revolution, individual judgment is made suspect.

Yet Chiang Kuei is no uncritical defender of the traditional ways. The novel also makes clear the tragedies which frequently resulted from arranged marriages: Liu Shao-ch'iao's marriage with Yeh P'in-hsia is the clearest example. In another case, the existence of sexual longing in the widowed Mrs. Hung and her satisfaction when it is gratified certainly go against the old Confucian tradition of chaste widowhood. But Chiang Kuei presents the woman's feelings as natural.

Chiang Kuei's verdict on the cultural revolution which China experienced during the first two decades of the twentieth century, then, is that it was necessary and justified but that it was carried too far. Its iconoclastic temper, when accepted uncritically, predisposed many young people to accept the apocalyptic vision of Communism.

CHAPTER 7

Swallow Tower

K ENG Tzu-hsiu, the hero, is the son of a revered revolutionary martyr and has been raised by his strong-willed mother in Shanghai. In these two conditions he resembles Hung T'ung-yeh, the protagonist of *The Two Suns*, but there the resemblance ends for Hung T'ung-yeh was brought up in poverty and Keng Tzu-hsiu received a sheltered upbringing and a college education. Although he was educated as a banker, his mother managed the family business enterprises until her death and Keng Tzu-hsiu did not acquire practical experience in any profession.

His mother arranged his marriage to his first cousin, an athletic young woman named Lan Wei-chen who was two years his senior and a few inches taller. Although husband and wife loved each other, Lan Wei-chen had a stronger personality and greater self-assurance and she was not content with the traditional domestic role. She took an active part in the Keng family business and later opened her own sporting equipment shop. Her surplus energy went into organizing a girls' basketball team which often went on tour as far afield as Southeast Asia.

Keng Tzu-hsiu feels inadequate in his wife's presence, and the love between them is more like that of an elder sister and younger brother than a man and his wife. In private, Wei-chen addresses her husband as Little Brother. After a time, Keng Tzu-hsiu decides to seek the maturity that is denied him in Shanghai by moving. Since his family holds a substantial portion of the stock of the Tsao-chuang Mining Company, he wangles a position as Branch Manager of the company's Hsüchow office. As the train pulls out of the Shanghai station, he is gratified by the rare sight of tears in Wei-chen's eyes.

A very different environment awaits him in Hsüchow. He is lionized because of his company position, personal wealth, and good looks. Even the formidable Jang Hua-t'ing, a powerful secret society leader and business man widely feared in Hsüchow, seeks his friendship and cooperation. Before he has been in Hsüchow very long, Keng Tzu-hsiu meets a prostitute called Hua Liu-pao who, at twenty-seven, is past her professional prime. He is told that she embraced coolies, smoked heroin, and had once served the bestial warlord Chang Tsung-ch'ang. When an employee seeks to curry favor with Keng Tzu-hsiu by sending Hua Liu-pao to his bedroom, Keng is furious, orders her from the room, and dashes a teacup to the floor. But when he has calmed down, he regrets his rudeness, seeks her out, embraces her, and buries his face in her hair.

Keng Tzu-hsiu learns that Hua Liu-pao had never served either coolies or General Chang Tsung-ch'ang—those stories were rumors spread by jealous rivals—and that although she had smoked heroin, she was not addicted. Although he refuses her sexual invitation, they sleep together, in an inverted "V" with heads together and bodies apart. Hua Liu-pao is impressed with the young man who treats her like a human being. Keng Tzu-hsiu's strongest feeling towards the woman, whose beauty is beginning to fade, is protectiveness. Although Hua Liu-pao is even taller than his wife Wei-chen, her lower station in life and her less aggressive personality allow him to feel dominant. These feelings, absent in his marital relationship, are entirely agreeable. He soon resolves to be Hua Liu-pao's friend, protector, and mentor, and urges her to strive for self-respect.

The first step is to change her name. Hua Liu-pao is merely her professional name. Keng Tzu-hsiu learns that her real surname is Yao and suggests that she call herself Yao Liu-hua.

Yao Liu-hua announces that she is giving up her life as a prostitute; she already had ceased to accept customers. Her new status is hard to define. When asked, Keng Tzu-hsiu calls her his girl friend but not his concubine, and allows others to believe that she is his wife. Her position is enhanced when Keng Tzu-hsiu becomes Jang Hua-t'ing's sworn brother and Jang Hua-t'ing's wife takes Yao Liu-hua as an adopted sister. The Jangs give her a legitimate job as manager of a restaurant and provide her with a fine residence. Yet she realizes that her good fortune and respectability depend entirely upon her association with Keng Tzu-hsiu.

When Wei-chen comes to Hsüchow to visit her husband, she learns of his association with Yao Liu-hua. She is disturbed at first, but accepts the situation and turns it to suit herself. An arrangement is made whereby Wei-chen will pay monthly visits to Hsüchow in hopes of conceiving a child and providing an heir for the Keng family. Meanwhile, Yao Liu-hua, with Wei-chen's full approval, will live with Keng Tzu-hsiu in Hsüchow and her status will not be that of a concubine, but of a second wife. If she becomes pregnant, the child will be recognized as belonging to the Keng family, and her own position will be assured. Wei-chen realizes that her husband needs someone to look after him; since her business demands her presence in Shanghai, she is happy to have Yao Liu-hua serve as second wife. As Wei-chen explains it to Keng Tzu-hsiu, a man may have both the flower (herself) and the leaf (Yao Liu-hua) or only the flower and all will be well, so long as he does not want only the leaf. Wei-chen takes Yao Liu-hua back to Shanghai for a thorough medical examination and a proper new wardrobe. When Yao Liu-hua returns to Keng in Hsüchow, they begin to live together as man and wife.

Yao Liu-hua cherishes the new life she has found in the Keng family and hopes that it will be permanent. Her former life as a prostitute seems safely behind her. Gradually she seems to gain self-confidence and self-respect.

One day Keng Tzu-hsiu and Yao Liu-hua ride out into the countryside in rickshas to visit the ancient dwellings known as the *Yentzu lou* (Swallow Tower). The Swallow Tower had been erected during the T'ang Dynasty by one Secretary Chang, an official of Hsüchow, in order to demonstrate his love for his concubine Kuan P'an-p'an. After his death, Kuan P'an-p'an had remained living alone at Swallow Tower for some fifteen years. The T'ang poet Po Chü-i had written a number of poems about Swallow Tower, and in one of them had made a slighting reference to Kuan P'an-p'an's refusal to follow her master in death. After that Kuan P'an-p'an had starved herself to death.

Yao Liu-hua grows depressed as Keng Tzu-hsiu helps her to read the poems on the walls of Swallow Tower. She feels faint and for a moment it seems to her that she is Kuan P'an-p'an and Keng Tzu-hsiu is Secretary Chang. Yao Liu-hua blames Po Chü-i for causing Kuan P'an-p'an to take her own life; at the same time she feels the concubine should have died shortly after her master's death.

The shadow of Swallow Tower remains in Yao Liu-hua's mind. She would like to forget her own past but the past will not forget her. When war comes, Yao Liu-hua attends the organizational meeting of a corps of volunteer nurses. A Communist agent, posing as the daughter of a respectable and scholarly family, sabotages the meeting by asking the other women if they are willing to associate with the former prostitute Hua Liu-pao. Humiliated, Yao Liu-hua flees in tears.

When Keng Tzu-hsiu receives accreditation as a war correspondent for a New York newspaper and travels through the areas controlled by Chinese puppet troops serving the Japanese Army in central China, Yao Liu-hua accompanies him. It is a trying but happy time for both of them. Keng Tzu-hsiu's first wife has just borne him a son, so she wants him to join her in Shanghai. But he is enjoying his peripatetic existence and does not want to return to domestic life. Using his duty—he is writing stories which will promote international sympathy for China—he defers any decision and his letters to his wife grow fewer and fewer. For her part, Yao Liu-hua enjoys having Keng Tzu-hsiu all to herself; if they go to Shanghai, she will have to share him with his wife, and her own position will be uncertain because she has not borne him a child.

While they are traveling in a puppet-controlled area north of Nanking, an officer recognizes Yao Liu-hua. He had slept with her ten years before in Hsüchow. That night he comes to her room and seeks entrance. He proves that he has known her before by recalling three birthmarks on her body, and asks if it wasn't she who had once served General Chang Tsung-ch'ang? Desperate, Yao Liu-hua tells him to come in, and when he does, she shoots him to death with her pistol. Her story that the officer tried to force his way into the room is accepted and the matter rests.

Keng Tzu-hsiu and Yao Liu-hua make their way to the headquarters of General Chang Tzu-chung who is preparing to cross the Han River and attack the Japanese in the Ta-hung Mountains. Keng Tzu-hsiu insists upon accompanying the troops into action. The commanders are reluctant to permit this, and when pressed by Keng, one explains that they are afraid he might get hurt. Since Keng Tzu-hsiu has been trying for several years to act the man, this infuriates him. When Yao Liu-hua timidly suggests that he might gather news just as well by remaining behind, he turns on her with a harsh rebuke; it is the first time he has spoken roughly to her in front of others.

In the end, both Keng Tzu-hsiu and Yao Liu-hua join the troops in the campaign which costs General Chang Tzu-chung his life in May, 1940. Keng Tzu-hsiu is shot in the leg and since it is sixty hours before he can be gotten to a medical aid station, his leg has to be amputated. The stump becomes infected and his condition grows worse.

Wei-chen arrives at the rear-area hospital in time to show her dying husband a photograph of his son and to be with him when he dies. His last words are: "Sister, please look after Liu-hua."

Meanwhile, Yao Liu-hua retires to her own room, determined not to repeat the mistake of the concubine Kuan P'an-p'an. Before putting a bullet through her brain, she carefully arranges certain precious articles on the table at the end of her bed. These are the date of the death of Keng Tzu-hsiu's father, embroidered on cloth and framed in metal, the poems copied by Keng Tzu-hsiu from the walls of Swallow Tower, the genealogical card which she had received from Jang Hua-t'ing's wife upon her adoption as a sister, and the box of silk stockings which Wei-chen had brought her as a gift. In the book of Swallow Tower poems, Wei-chen and Keng Tzu-hsiu's younger brother Tzu-chi find the following inscription by Yao Liu-hua:

In former times at T'ungshan [Hsüchow] I came to the Swallow Tower with Tzu-hsiu, and read the poems of P'an-p'an. I understood deeply how P'an-p'an, as a concubine, should not have returned to live alone in the tower for as long as ten years after the Secretary's death. If I had been P'an-p'an, then Tzu-hsiu would assuredly have been my Secretary. Since the Secretary died, and the Secretary could not return, my affairs would have been finished. This poem, in imitation of P'an-p'an:
Reluctantly, she looks toward the empty room in remorse,
Blushing like the camellia after spring has gone.
One doesn't ask that things turn out so fittingly as this:
I willingly go to the underworld with you.[1]

Wei-chen and Tzu-chi recognize the spirit in which Yao Liu-hua has taken her own life although such a spirit is foreign to their own natures.

"I can't say she was wrong to die. Only such thoughts and emotions are really too old-fashioned."[2]

Wei-chen also realizes that Keng Tzu-hsiu's death was unnecessary and that in a sense both have died out of a rather romantic desire to justify themselves.

"I can't blame her; she learned Tzu-hsiu's lesson, her feelings ran too deep. All his life Tzu-hsiu had too much emotion and not enough firmness." [3]

But then Wei-chen feels that these words are too harsh and she murmurs:

"No, no, I shouldn't say that of him. Since matters have come to such a pass, what's the use of my speaking of him? He sacrificed himself for the country, isn't that good, surely? Liu-hua—her end was still more rare of attainment, a rare death!" [4]

Keng Tzu-chi has the last word in the discussion.

"Very well, sister. But let those whom we see before us be the last generation to be influenced by Kuan P'an-p'an and Swallow Tower, and that will be well enough." [5]

The changing times, Chiang Kuei is saying, are sweeping away characters like those of Keng Tzu-hsiu and Yao Liu-hua.

Not long after *Swallow Tower's* serial publication in the *China Daily* had concluded with the death of Keng Tzu-hsiu and the suicide of Yao Liu-hua, a colonel whom Chiang Kuei knew accosted him on the street and said, "You mustn't treat that Sixth Miss so cruelly," referring to the death of Yao Liu-hua. But Chiang Kuei considered her death a merciful one.

Her all came from Keng Tzu-hsiu; if she lost Keng Tzu-hsiu, she lost everything. If she had not committed suicide but had gone back to Shanghai with Wei-chen, her position in the Keng household would at best have been that of another P'u-k'ou-lu Ah-i [a longtime family servant of Lan Wei-chen—TAR]. The years and months ahead of her would have been long, and she could never have forgotten those unendurable insults given her by Shih Yün-liang and by the Niao River Mutual Security Head. She feared that she might not be able to rank as the second P'u-k'ou-lu Ah-i. The lack of sympathy could not be made good, and disgrace should have

an end. If the author in a moment of feeling for the character he has
created with his own hand had let her go on living, this on the contrary
would have been cruel.[6]

It is consistent with Chiang Kuei's view of human nature that no
one is perfect. Every character, however attractive, has some flaw
and falls short in some way. Given this view, his conclusion about
Yao Liu-hua is quite realistic.

The key to Chiang Kuei's endorsement of Yao Liu-hua's suicide
is to be found in his own experience. He considers the novel
Swallow Tower to be his masterpiece. It was written during the
period when he faced a prison sentence and it contains the attitude
which he acquired out of his painful experience.

China has a saying: "A gentleman may be killed, but he may not be
humiliated." Having gotten involved in successive pitfalls, I have a new
way of looking at human life and society. According to this new point of
view, which has sunk deeply into me, I have written another novel called
Swallow Tower. This is my "real work"; I consider its worth far above that
of *The Whirlwind*.[7]

Chiang Kuei's post-1961 autobiographical writings contain many
references to his ordeal before the law.

It wasted much of my spirit, it gave me a headful of white hair, and the still
more obvious "result" was that it seems to have made the false become the
true; it planted firmly upon me a little queue. This little queue has its obvious uses for little men of the second and third classes, they can grasp it in
their hands at any time, hold it tightly. When there is need to "drop stones
on a man who has fallen down a well," they don't need to arrange matters
beforehand; it takes only a "knowing little smile" and then everything is
accomplished.[8]

The new attitude of Chiang Kuei which is expressed in *Swallow
Tower* is that when one has a shameful episode in one's
past—regardless of whether or not one was at fault—society will not
allow one to rise above it and make a new life of happiness and
fulfillment. Chiang Kuei seems to feel that although he was without
guilt in his wife's death, the ordeal marked him permanently. His
final acquittal did not erase the events of three years.

His fatalistic recognition of the past's power over the present is expressed in *Swallow Tower* through the former prostitute Yao Liu-hua. Yet the novel does not end on this note. As Chiang Kuei wrote in the afterword to *Swallow Tower*:

Today's social conditions and those of before the war are two different worlds. It is vain to recall, and moreover it is profitless. In the first years of the Republic, the kneelings-in-obeisance, the little feet, the queue hanging down behind the head, of which the old men were so fond, finally disappeared, and this caused them the greatest regret; one by one they departed from a world in which they could not fit. Whenever in history there are social changes caused by war and disorder, there are always some dregs, numerous or few, which sink to the bottom; that cannot be reckoned a tragedy.[9]

With the passing of old-fashioned people such as Keng Tzu-hsiu and Yao Liu-hua, more modern and practical people such as Lan Wei-chen and Keng Tzu-chi step forward confidently to carry on life. Wei-chen returns to Shanghai to raise Tzu-hsiu's child and Tzu-chi, breaking with tradition, chooses his own future bride. Like Lin Tu at the conclusion of *Breaking Free*, they turn their backs upon the past to face the challenges of their contemporary world.

CHAPTER 8

The Lesser Novels and Miscellaneous Writings

THE four novels which Chiang Kuei regards as his serious literary work have been discussed in the preceding chapters. This chapter is concerned with the author's lesser novels and other writings.

The first three novels discussed here may be called the Taiwan Novels, since all three are set in Taiwan. *Ch'un-ch'eng* (Spring City), *Chu-men feng-yü* (Turmoil among the Prosperous), and *Fen ch'ing-chi* (Burnt Memory) are not considered serious works by their author. Certainly the first, and probably the other two as well, were written as "pot-boilers."

The fourth novel, *Hsi-yen* (The Wedding Feast), is set on the Chinese mainland. In quality, it is about equal to the three Taiwan Novels. Its theme, like that of *Spring City*, is patriotic: both novels were serialized in the government newspaper, the *Central Daily News*. It is doubtful if the author regards it very highly.

Included under the heading of "miscellaneous writings" are two short stories, three autobiographical pieces, a brief autobiography, an historical-biographical study, and a reminiscence. Finally, a brief section from Chiang Kuei's projected trilogy of novels is described.

I Spring City

The hero of *Spring City* is a penniless young refugee named Cheng T'ung-chi. Cheng, formerly a teacher on the mainland and a guerrilla fighter during the War of Resistance against Japan, is a staunch anti-Communist but not directly involved in politics. His only friend is his former guerrilla commander, Kao Lan-chih, a bluff and hearty old soldier.

Living in the south of the island, Cheng T'ung-chi falls in with a

Taiwanese named Hu Lao-nai. Hu, who was conscripted during the war by the Japanese, owns a house and an orchard and is the head of a large family but makes his real living as head of a gang of nighttime rustlers who butcher other people's cattle in the fields and sell the beef to local restaurants. Although he realizes he is not cut out for a life of crime, Cheng allows himself to become a member of Hu Lao-nai's gang because no one else has shown any particular interest in him. He lets his hair grow long, goes barefoot, drinks heavily, and lets himself go to seed.

The regenerating influence which rescues Cheng T'ung-chi is a Taiwanese girl, Sheng A-to, who has been disowned by her ill-tempered mother and has no home. Kao Lan-chih befriends her and places her with Cheng T'ung-chi, who at least has a simple squatter's shack. The girl's presence reawakens Cheng's sense of self-respect. He breaks off his life of crime and finds honest work as an employee of a paint factory. Sheng A-to learns to be a seamstress and soon operates her own flourishing shop. Cheng T'ung-chi, through frugality and diligence, rises to become an independent painting contractor. The couple eventually fall in love and become life partners, although formal marriage is deferred until they can win the approval of Sheng A-to's mother.

After 468 pages, Cheng T'ung-chi and Sheng A-to are a prosperous couple with numerous thriving business concerns. Hu Lao-nai, having run afoul of the law, repents of his life of crime and after serving a reasonable sentence, goes into the honest business of selling fruit. In time he joins Cheng T'ung-chi as one of his business partners. Sheng A-to is reconciled with her mother who is led to believe that Cheng T'ung-chi is a wealthy suitor and at last a formal marriage takes place. By that time, the long hoped-for event is a reality: Sheng A-to is pregnant with their first child.

Although propagandistic in its stress upon the unity of Taiwanese and mainlander in the effort for economic growth in Taiwan, the novel is entertaining and readable because it concerns likable characters struggling for worthwhile goals. Sheng A-to is one of Chiang Kuei's most appealing female characters. The dark and ironic vision which dominates Chiang Kuei's serious novels is absent from *Spring City*. The closest thing to a negative character is a mainlander intellectual who writes carping essays about the lack of political freedom on Taiwan until exposure to Cheng T'ung-chi teaches him the value of hard, practical work, and he stops criticizing and becomes a school teacher in the countryside.

II   Turmoil among the Prosperous

Turmoil among the Prosperous, published in 1967 by *Lien-ho t'u-shu kung-ssu* (United Library Company) in *Sheng-huo tsa-chih hsiao-shuo tsung-shu* (Life Magazine Fiction Collection) is a story about a poor little rich girl. Yang Hsin-i, seventeen, is the daughter of a wealthy mainlander businessman in some unnamed southern city on Taiwan. She has had to overcome the loneliness of a pampered only child and the jealousy of her less fortunate schoolmates and has achieved first place in her Middle School class. Although she has two close friends of her own age, she is troubled by the mysterious tension evident between her parents. In fact, her mother correctly suspects her father of carrying on a love affair with another woman. When the truth finally comes out, the father flees to South America with his lover, never to return. Since he has looted his numerous commercial enterprises before departure, his wife and daughter face bankruptcy and creditors' lawsuits and are left poor. However, at the end of the novel, the help of friends makes it possible for Yang Hsin-i to fulfill her dream of attending college and preparing herself for a career in medicine.

The most interesting feature of this novel is the subplot involving Yang Hsin-i's friend, Sang Ming-sang, and her mother. During the war on Taiwan, Sang Ming-sang's mother, then a young woman, was seduced by an unscrupulous doctor, became his mistress, and bore him three children. Sang Ming-sang was the eldest; she had two brothers. After a time, the doctor married a wealthy but vicious woman and discarded his mistress and her children. When Sang Ming-sang's mother demanded more money than the doctor was prepared to give her and made a nuisance of herself, his new wife, Pin Yü-huan, who was involved in many criminal activities, sent a man who threw acid into the face of Sang Ming-sang's mother as she slept. Disfigured for life, Sang Ming-sang's mother took her children and fled to the south. She made no complaint to the police and became a recluse. Years later when Sang Ming-sang was in Middle School, she learned that Pin Yü-huan had hired a young man to ruin her face as her mother's had been ruined and to lead her brothers into a life of crime. Pin Yü-huan's plot failed when the youth chosen for this mission fell in love with Sang Ming-sang and eventually killed Pin Yü-huan, her husband, and himself. The more extravagant touches aside, Chiang Kuei's description of the struggles of Sang Ming-sang's mother to survive and keep her children alive in a world in which she has almost no resources and no one to turn to for help is moving. The picture is one of a society in which money, friends, and connections count for much, and law, police, and courts count for little or nothing.

III   Burnt Memory

In 1968, the United Library Company published a second novel by Chiang Kuei entitled *Burnt Memory*. The heroine is Yang Wu-ch'üan, only daughter of the author Yang Feng, an influential poet at the time of the May Fourth Movement. After emigrating to Taiwan, Yang Feng settled in Taipei and became a highly successful author in the knight-errant genre, which Chiang Kuei has always disdained. I San-cheng, a cousin of Yang Wu-ch'üan from a wealthy family in Hong Kong, comes to Taiwan to receive a Chinese education and lives with the Yangs. Under Yang Feng's policy of benign neglect, the two adolescent cousins become lovers. Yang Wu-ch'üan becomes pregnant twice and both pregnancies are terminated by abortion. When she becomes pregnant for a third time, they wish to marry, but—family objections aside—the fact that the youth has college and obligatory military service ahead of him makes marriage impossible. Yang Wu-ch'üan entices an established businessman into marrying her before the pregnancy becomes apparent, but when he discovers that she is not a virgin, he abandons her in Hong Kong and leaves for parts unknown. She returns to Taiwan and has an abortion. Later she becomes the mistress and confederate of a notorious criminal, who arranges for her to be the logical suspect when he murders a former mistress. Yang Wu-ch'üan suffers three years' confinement—without trial, since there is not enough evidence to convict her—before the murderer's wife brings the truth to the attention of the police. Released, she refuses I San-cheng's offer of marriage for she feels that she has flouted society's codes too long and does not deserve a normal, happy future.

IV The Wedding Feast

The Wedding Feast, which was published in serial form in the *Central Daily News*, is set in the author's native Shantung Province. It is a romance of the warlord period and reaches its climax as the Kuomintang's Northern Expedition delivers north China from the oppression of the warlords.

Ch'iu Hsin-fu, born in the last years of the Ch'ing Dynasty, is a victim of the traditional family system. His father denies his wish to attend a modern school and when he reaches the age of sixteen, his parents choose a bride for him. The bride, Kao Yüeh-lan, is nine years her husband's senior, sturdy, industrious, intelligent, and properly submissive to her husband and his parents. But she is not the bride Ch'iu Hsin-fu would have chosen for himself.

Ch'iu Hsin-fu and Kao Yüeh-lan have two children: a boy, Huai-an, and a girl, Huai-ying. After his parents die, Ch'iu Hsin-fu realizes that although he has some inherited property, he has no trade. He decides to set up and operate an inn. With the help of an older and more experienced employee, Ch'iu Hsin-fu becomes the proprietor of the Star of Wealth Inn. Kao Yüeh-lan, glad of an opportunity to show that she can do something besides cook, becomes the very capable business manager.

Ch'iu Hsin-fu spends every night with his wife but he has never been able to carry on a normal conversation with her. Their conversations are carried on through Magpie, Kao Yüeh-lan's maid. Ch'iu Hsin-fu daydreams of romance with Magpie or with Chang Lan-hua, the daughter of his restaurant manager.

When Huai-an and Huai-ying complete primary school, Ch'iu Hsin-fu is determined to send them to the Middle School in the provincial capital city of Tsinan. Kao Yüeh-lan objects because she feels that they ought to learn the family business. Ch'iu Hsin-fu absents himself from home for a few days and Kao Yüeh-lan, at her wits' end, is glad to let her husband have his way.

After Middle School in Tsinan, Huai-an enters engineering school while Huai-ying enrolls in a medical school for girls. Huai-an is befriended by an older schoolmate, Chung Hsiang, and through Chung Hsiang, Huai-an and Huai-ying enter the circle of a local educator and newspaper editor named Lo T'ung-sheng. Lo T'ung-sheng is a member of the Kuomintang and his mission is to attract likely youths into the party. Because his wife is the daughter of a formerly eminent warlord, Lo T'ung-sheng is on good terms with the warlords and enjoys many useful contacts. Huai-an and Huai-ying meet Wang Shih-chia, a retired but extremely influential member of the Peiyang (Northern) clique of major warlords. Wang Shih-chia recognizes that the day of the warlords is done and that the Kuomintang's victory means a brighter future for China. He exerts his influence to forward the revolutionary activities of Lo T'ung-sheng.

In the late nineteen-twenties, times are hard in north China. Banditry flourishes and the roads are unsafe for travelers. The fields of tall kaoliang, twice a man's height, furnish a superb refuge for the bandits. The local villagers organize United Hamlet Associations to defend themselves. Troops, attached to one or another of the local warlords, are poorly paid and poorly disciplined and sometimes worse than the bandits. Indeed, it is frequently hard to tell the troops from the bandits.

One day in summer, mounted and heavily armed men appear in Ch'iu Hsin-fu's village and quarter themselves at his inn. After their departure, mounted and armed cavalrymen appear and accuse Ch'iu Hsin-fu of harboring bandits. Their leader demands a large sum of money or Ch'iu Hsin-fu will be arrested and taken away. As it happens, Ch'iu Hsin-fu has been dreaming of leaving his home and traveling and impulsively he volunteers to go with the troops. When they ride off, Ch'iu Hsin-fu disappears with them. Inquiries prove fruitless and for years not a word is heard of him.

Ch'iu Huai-ying's roommate at the girls' medical school is Tung Jen-fang. Tung Jen-fang, originally reticent about her family, finally confides in Huai-ying.

Tung Chan-piao was a ne'er-do-well gambler and ruffian. He married Hua Ching-hsien, who watched helplessly as he gambled and drank away his property. As they faced penury, the wife learned that a couple from a distant province were seeking lodgings, for the woman was about to give birth. Hua Ching-hsien persuaded Tung Chan-piao to sell them his house, and the traveler, Tu Chin-sheng, permitted the Tungs to stay on in the house.

Shortly, the traveler fell ill and died. His wife gave birth to a son. At about the same time, Hua Ching-hsien gave birth to a daughter, Jen-fang. When Tung Chan-piao demanded the remaining money from Hua Ching-hsien and she refused, he struck her unconscious, took the money, and ran away.

Tu Chin-sheng's widow revived Hua Ching-hsien and, since Hua Ching-hsien's milk was insufficient, nursed the baby girl herself. When her own son died, Tu Chin-sheng's widow and Hua Ching-hsien shared the care of the girl and managed to support themselves by doing seamstress work.

When Jen-fang was about eight, Tung Chan-piao reappeared. He had become a division commander. He forced his wife and Tu Chin-sheng's attractive widow to come away with him by threatening to kill them and burn down their neighborhood if they refused.

Once reunited with her husband, Hua Ching-hsien found that her economic problems were over and she began to put some money aside. But Tung Jen-fang found that her fellow students in the Middle School sneered at her behind her back because her father was a notorious warlord.

Tung Chan-piao demanded that Tu Chin-sheng's widow become his concubine. The unfortunate woman attempted suicide six times to avoid his embraces. Finally Tung Jen-fang and Tu Chin-sheng's widow determined to escape Tung Chan-piao's control. They went to Tsinan and sent word that Tu Chin-sheng's widow had an incapacitating illness; Tung Jen-fang was nursing her. Tung Chan-piao let them alone, and Tung Jen-fang enrolled in medical school, pretending to be the daughter of a merchant.

The Revolutionary Army of the Kuomintang approaches Shantung and the warlords prepare for the showdown battle. Lo T'ung-sheng assigns Huai-an as liaison officer between the undercover Kuomintang organization in Shantung and the cavalry division headed by one of Tung Chan-piao's subordinate commanders, Chao Erh-ch'eng, who is preparing to defect to the Revolutionary Army. Ch'iu Huai-ying joins an older male physician in setting up a field hospital corps to care for the wounded of Chao Erh-ch'eng's division.

The Revolutionary Army is victorious. In the aftermath, Tung Chan-piao is beheaded by his own superior. Ch'iu Huai-an discovers that his father, missing for years, is a lieutenant in the Revolutionary Army. Father, son, and daughter are reunited.

Ch'iu Hsin-fu had escaped the bandits sometime after learning that the bandits who had visited his inn were soldiers in disguise and had made his way to the south where he enlisted in the Revolutionary Army. His immediate superior was Chung Hsiang, who had been his son's friend in Tsinan.

A new and brighter day dawns for the people of north China as the last of the warlords are swept away by the Revolutionary Army. Vanishing, too, are the outdated ways of the past such as arranged marriages. Ch'iu Hsin-fu has determined that his own son and daughter shall choose their own mates; he is glad to learn that Huai-an is to marry Tung Jen-fang and that Chung Hsiang's proposal has been accepted by Huai-ying. He himself has learned, during his years of separation from his wife, that Kao Yüeh-lan is his true love after all.

Since the twenty-fifth wedding anniversary of Ch'iu Hsin-fu and Kao Yüeh-lan is approaching, they decide that three ceremonies will be performed at the same time. Preparations are made for a lavish wedding celebration at the Star of Wealth Inn. Ch'iu Hsin-fu and Kao Yüeh-lan repeat their original marriage vows and their son and daughter are married to the partners of their own choice.

V Short Stories

Between 1961 and 1964, Chiang Kuei wrote ten short stories which were published in various newspapers and magazines in Taiwan and Hong Kong, and later collected and published in book form under the title *Six Month Frost* by the Wen-hsin Bookstore in Tainan in 1969. Unfortunately this book quickly went out of print and the Wen-hsin Bookstore went out of business. Only two of these short stories have been available for this study.

"*Pu-ho chiao-ti hsieh-tzu*" (The Shoe That Didn't Fit) appeared in the bilingual Hong Kong magazine *Chung-wai hua-pao* (Cosmorama). This light short story concerns middle-aged Hsieh Ling-ti, an emigrant from the mainland who has never married. He recalls that when he was a child, his parents had bought him a pair of new leather shoes which pinched his feet. His kindly father had allowed him to discard them in favor of his worn and comfortable cloth shoes.

One day Hsieh Ling-ti sees a beautiful woman walking past his shop. He falls in love with her on the spot. Through careful inquiries, he learns her name but, at the same time, that she is married and far beyond his economic and social reach in any case.

He gets drunk and his shop assistants carry him upstairs to bed. Dimly, he senses a female presence entering his room. Believing that it is the object of his infatuation, he grabs his visitor and begins to mutter romantic nonsense to her. In fact, his visitor is the aged and sharp-tongued woman who manages his household and she promptly boxes his ears and begins to scold him.

The other short story, "Ah-yüan," appeared in the December 1961 issue of *Tso-p'in* (Opus) magazine. Restrained, somber, and frightening, it is far different from "The Shoe That Didn't Fit."

Chang Ssu-liu is a refugee from the Chinese mainland. Once he had had property, a wife, and three children. He had flown to Taiwan from the mainland with his small daughter Hsin-pao. His wife and his two sons, with the cash which represented the family's property, had embarked on the steamer *T'ai-p'ing* and the *T'ai-p'ing* was lost at sea; no one survived. Chang Ssu-liu found himself alone, but for Hsin-pao, and penniless in Taiwan. He got a clerical job and rented a small house on the outskirts of the city where there was less danger from traffic for his daughter at play. Hsin-pao means everything to him; she is all he has to live for.

One day Chang Ssu-liu sees an attractive woman of his own age walking near his home. He learns that her name is Ah-yüan and that she resides in a nearby Buddhist temple. Gradually they become friends and he learns that her husband and children also had gone down on the *T'ai-p'ing*. Ah-yüan becomes very fond of Hsin-pao, who is about to enter first grade, and pays for an artist to come and give the child drawing lessons.

Chang Ssu-liu's landlady has an adolescent daughter who is insane but apparently harmless. She sits on the wall grinning at passersby in a disconcerting way or runs after them clutching at their sleeves. This girl shows an interest in the drawing lessons and is allowed to take part. She is quite skillful.

When Chang Ssu-liu proposes marriage to Ah-yüan, she declines, saying that marriage is out of the question for her. Chang, dejected, returns to his house and drinks himself to the point of courage; then he forces his way into the Buddhist temple and begs Ah-yüan to marry him. She rejects him coldly. He returns home and falls asleep.

The next morning, contrite, he makes his way to the temple to apologize, only to learn that Ah-yüan has departed. She has left him her considerable fortune to be used for Hsin-pao's education.

Chang returns home and finds the landlady's mad daughter kneeling by Hsin-pao's bed. Her hands are locked about his daughter's neck and the little girl is dead. Chang wrenches the mad girl away from his daughter and then drops to the floor in a faint. The mad girl stands looking at him with her strange grin.

VI *Nonfiction Writings*

Since the publication of *The Two Suns* in 1961, Chiang Kuei has written a number of short nonfiction pieces which have been published in various magazines and newspapers in Taiwan. Most have been autobiographical.

In November 1961 Chiang Kuei's essay *"Pai-fa"* (White Hair) appeared in the journal *Opus*. It was written shortly after the death of the author's wife. The theme is how difficult and painful experiences have caused the author's hair gradually to turn gray.

The essay begins by recounting the death of the author's twelve-year-old daughter Mei of an illness in 1944. In that year, the Japanese Army in China launched a major offensive and Chiang Kuei and his family had to flee to the west. They sailed upstream on the Han River to Yun-yang where they remained in safety. The essay describes their postwar life in Shanghai, their flight to Taiwan in December 1948, and the failure of the business in Tainan. Bankruptcy left the author and his family in desperate poverty. The essay describes in detail the many hardships of the job as the caretaker of a Roman Catholic church on the outskirts of Tainan and the disagreeable character of his employer. Finally, after seven years, Chiang Kuei quit his job and moved his family into other quarters. The essay concludes with the death of his wife.

The essay *"Wo-ti chia-shih ho t'ung-nien"* (My Family and Youth) appeared in the February 1963 issue of *Opus*. Subtitled "A Chapter of an Autobiography," the essay is a rambling account of Chiang Kuei's family, childhood, and youth in the ancestral town of Hsiang-chou Chen in Chu-ch'eng hsien in Shantung Province.

In the March 1963 issue of *Opus*, Chiang Kuei continued his autobiography with a second chapter entitled *"Chi-nan liang-nien"* (Two Years in Tsinan). This essay recalls the two years which the author spent as a student at the First Provincial Middle School in Tsinan.

These essays confirmed what some Chinese critics, who were familiar with Shantung in the 1920s, had guessed: that *The Whirlwind* was to some extent autobiographical, that the Fang clan represented an actual family, and that the characters Fang Hsiang-ch'ien and Fang T'ung-san, at least, represented real people.

The essays, anecdotal like much of the author's fiction, not only shed much light on his sources but provide interesting records of Chinese social history.

The short "Chiang Kuei *tzu-chuan*" (Chiang Kuei's Autobiography) appeared in the September 1969 issue of the journal *Hsin-hsia* (Neo-Cathay). It is a straightforward account of his life, with about two-thirds of the space devoted to the period after 1949.

A much longer historical-biographical narrative, "*Feng-pao lang-ya*" (Stormy Shantung), appeared in fifty-seven installments in *China Daily News* in 1972.

The first part of this essay is an historical account of the republican revolutionary movement in Shantung Province before and after the overthrow of the Ch'ing Dynasty in 1911. The revolutionaries whom Chiang Kuei discusses were mostly members of Dr. Sun Yat-sen's T'ung Meng Hui before the 1911 Revolution. After the new government of the Republic of China fell into the ruthless hands of President Yuan Shih-k'ai, many of them fought on against him. The essay recounts the events described in chapter one of this study and culminates with the uprising in Chu-ch'eng city and its suppression in February 1912. It also contains capsule biographies of about a dozen revolutionary leaders of Shantung Province.

In the second part of the essay, Chiang Kuei presents the biographies of numerous members of the Wang clan including his father Wang Ming-k'o, his father's younger brother Wang Ming-shao, his widow Miss Jen Lan-yin, and Wang Hsiang-ch'ien. This essay gives a fuller and more detailed account of Chiang Kuei's family background than any of the earlier autobiographical writings.

In the essay "*Shang-shih yü kan-chiu*" (Mortally Wounded and

Thinking of the Past) which appeared in the weekly literary supplement of the *Tu-li wan-pao* (Independent Evening News) on June 4, 1972, Chiang Kuei recalled the war years and commemorated an old friend. It is an account of his wartime tour across central China from Fifth War Area headquarters in Lao-ho-k'ou in northern Hupei Province to the outskirts of enemy-held Nanking and back again. His faithful companion on the journey was Tseng Shao-hua who had remained on the mainland after 1949. Recalling his friend's upright character, Chiang Kuei expressed his hope that he had been able to survive under Communist rule.

The essay *"Chen-ch'eng yü tzu-yu"* (Sincerity and Freedom) which appeared in the December 1969 issue of *Neo-Cathay* discussed sincerity and freedom in a totalitarian society in a rather disillusioned tone. The person who took these appealing qualities too seriously and attempted to speak with sincerity and act with freedom was likely to find himself in trouble. The establishment appreciated the uses of "sincerity" and "freedom" as masks to conceal the reality of oppression, but the actual exercise of sincerity and freedom would be tolerated only up to a point. Therefore the writer ought to be cautious and prudent and leave much unsaid.

VII   Excerpt from the Projected Trilogy

"T'ao-hua wan" (Spring Freshets) was published in the December 1972 issue of *Chung-hua ch'ing-nien* (Chinese Youth Quarterly). It is a section of Chiang Kuei's projected trilogy of novels, *Annals of a Prosperous Age.* "Spring Freshets" appears to be from the early part of the first novel of the trilogy, *Ch'ou-ch'ang huang-ho* (The Sorrow of the Yellow River).

As outlined by Chiang Kuei, the first novel is set in Shantung Province, north of Tsinan, along the Yellow River. A wealthy member of the gentry, Mr. X, is at a loss when the civil service examinations are abolished in 1905, and the last emperor of the Ch'ing Dynasty abdicates in 1912. The May Fourth Movement of 1919 weakens his paternal authority over his sons, who go their own ways. The major theme is change: the conflict between a dying tradition and the disturbing new ways.

The second novel of the trilogy, provisionally entitled *Ssu-hai wei chia* (Anywhere Is Home), is set in Hopei, Shantung, and Honan

Provinces between 1937 and 1949, and its major theme is the dislocation wrought by war. The sons of Mr. X follow many paths: collaborating with the Japanese, fighting for the National Government in Chungking, fighting for the Communists; some speculate and grow rich, while one organizes his own nonpartisan guerrilla force and grows so strong that he is courted by all sides. Mr. X joins the puppet regime in Peking in hopes that he can help to maintain the Chinese cultural tradition. In the eight years of war, everyone is uprooted and has to make the best of it; the Chinese people exhibit their endurance and resiliency.

The trilogy concludes with *P'iao-miao hsien-hsiang* (The Wonderland), which is set in Taiwan during the decade after 1949. There, cast upon their own resources, Mr. X and some of his sons struggle to survive with animal instinct. Finally tired of a world he can no longer understand, Mr. X takes his own life. China has passed through a difficult time, but her innate strength and adaptability promise that in the future she will recover her former greatness.

The "spring freshets" of the title of the excerpt is a reference to the first spring tides which sweep down the Yellow River. Three times a year—in spring, summer, and autumn—the Yellow River floodtides come and the officials responsible for flood control summon the workers of the village of Nan-hsia-wa to rebuild the dikes. This work is their only source of income; during the winter they nearly starve.

From time to time the more adventurous of the younger villagers leave to seek their fortunes elsewhere. But old Li Wu Tieh-tieh (Daddy Li the Fifth), who has never known any other life and takes poverty for granted, feels that it is better to remain in Nan-hsia-wa, because who knows what awaits one outside? His own son had struck out, taking his wife but leaving his son Ta-hsiang with old Li; nothing was heard for five years. Then came a letter from Man-chou-li on the border between Manchuria and Russia reporting that Li's son had died in Russia of illness and that the wife had remarried.

Li and his wife raise Ta-hsiang. The old woman denies herself food and warm clothing so that the boy can grow up healthy and strong. When the boy Ta-hsiang is fifteen, she dies. Ta-hsiang tells his grandfather that he is determined to leave Nan-hsia-wa, but he promises to remain while his grandfather is alive.

The spring floodtides that year are unusually heavy. The men labor through the night, building up the dikes and filling sandbags. According to legend, the river demands a human life and in the past human sacrifices had been made to it, but that had not been done for many years. Old Li makes a careless step on the dike and is swept away to his death. The crest passes and the waters are pacified.

Ta-hsiang realizes there is nothing holding him in Nan-hsia-wa, gets his meager belongings together, and sets out, vowing never to look upon the Yellow River again as long as he lives.

CHAPTER 9

Conclusion

C HINA in the nineteen-twenties and thirties reached her low point of degradation, humiliation, and confusion. Scorned by the Powers, and even by Japan, plague-ridden, famine-stricken, her masses ignorant and her intelligentsia searching among a host of foreign doctrines, she wallowed like a drifting hulk. Yen Fu, late in the nineteenth century, had felt China's weakness acutely and had wondered if it might not be a kind of racial inferiority. By the first decades of the twentieth century, the problem was more sharply posed by Ch'en Tu-hsiu. Would China sink beneath the burden of her past? Would she go the way of other degraded and decadent peoples unequal to the challenge of the times? Or would she make herself new and live? Ch'en Tu-hsiu saw clearly that the problem was cultural; without a thoroughgoing cultural change, a political revolution was meaningless—it merely replaced the Ch'ing emperor with Yuan Shih-k'ai. What was needed was to oust Confucius from his temple, to destroy the old and replace it with the new. Ch'en Tu-hsiu called upon the nation's youth to shed the dead ways of the past and become vital, aggressive, cosmopolitan, enlightened.

The New Culture Movement, which preceded the May Fourth Movement, was a tremendous liberating influence upon a generation of Chinese youth. Writers of that period, armed with the supple and responsive instrument of the *pai-hua,* turned to attack the tottering pillars of an outworn tradition. During this period, creative writers enjoyed much freedom. Challenging areas of subject matter lay before them. They might, like Chiang Kuei's uncle Wang T'ung-chao, write of the life and sufferings of the peasants under the irresponsible rule of the warlords, or like Yü Ta-fu in *Sinking* and Ting Ling in *Miss Sophie's Diary,* explore their own psyches in the confessional story. There were many targets to be attacked in tragic or satiric vein: the traditional family system with its arranged marriages, concubinage, and tyranny of the old over the young, the hypocrisy and obscurantism of the old moral codes, and the lack of social consciousness and cohesion.

The attack, over a period of years, was successful. The tradition, generally called Confucian, was dying or dead. What would take its place was not yet clear. Western liberalism, with its freedom of thought and individualism, appealed to those who understood it, but offered no very workable answers for China's desperate needs. The Kuomintang, after 1924, offered a nationalistic program of independence and unity leading to a sort of guided democracy and economic egalitarianism under Dr. Sun Yat-sen's Three Principles of the People. The Communist Party, small in numbers but rich in doctrine, offered, as Joseph Levenson has suggested, a total worldview which explained China's problems and promised solutions.

The position of the writer of fiction in traditional Chinese society had been marginal since his art was not considered a serious one. Although his role was probably more respectable in the twentieth century, the writers of Republican China still must have felt keenly their isolation. The intellectuals in Chinese society have long been a class apart from the common people to a degree not found in the West—witness the continuing efforts of the Chinese Communists to erase the distinction between mental and manual laborers. This sense of isolation, in the case of a writer, would be increased by the personal isolation imposed by creative work. Many must have wondered to what point they were laboring. To create a work of serious literature is difficult at best. Why—especially when people were suffering and starving all around—should one bother? Did one have the moral right to pursue even serious literary aims in the face of such suffering? Could they, as Wang Jen-shu asked in his afterword to *Breaking Free*, cultivate refinement in isolation?

For some, Communism offered a way out of this painful dilemma. Ting Ling, a writer of intensely personal stories of modern, liberated youth, and her husband Hu Yeh-p'in found that the Communist Party gave them an invigorating sense of mission. Moreover, it wanted them as writers and its ideology afforded a new perspective on literary work. The Communist Party, unlike the Kuomintang, took literature seriously and devoted painstaking efforts to winning control of the literary world. However, the Communist theory of creative writing was very different from that generally held by writers of the West or of Republican China.

The Communists denied the existence of a human nature common to all men. Instead, members of each social class possessed a distinctive class nature. By the same token, there was no such thing as art in general; there was only the art of this social class or that. The class struggle between the workers, peasants, and soldiers—the people—and their exploiters—the bourgeoisie—left no middle ground; the writer must take his stand and write for one class camp or the other.

The creative writer should not seek the wellsprings of creativity within himself, but among the masses who were his public. He should immerse himself completely in their life, becoming, insofar as possible, one with them. Out of his familiarity with them, a work of literature expressing their experience might arise. Such a work should inspire and arouse love and admiration for the people and hatred and contempt for the class enemies.

Such a philosophy of literature is at odds with assumptions generally held throughout the non-Communist world, and held even by certain Soviet Russian authors, but it has not meant the death of literary art in Communist China. As several studies—Roderick MacFarquhar's examination of the Hundred Flowers Period, for example—have shown, the old humanistic ideas about the independence of artistic creativity and autonomy of literature die very hard. But the controls are there, and had Chiang Kuei remained on the mainland in 1948 and somehow escaped the consequences of his landlord family background, he could not have written the sort of novels described in this study.

On Taiwan, he has had freedom to write, although perhaps not to write as freely as he would prefer. This freedom was the freedom of neglect. No one helped him write *The Whirlwind*, nor did the anti-Communist government on Taiwan reward him for writing that deeply anti-Communist novel. Later on, he was free to accept or reject the propagandistic *Spring City* assignment from the *Central Daily News;* it was poverty and the specter of starvation which drove him to that disagreeable task, not political compulsion. In the same way, he was free to write and publish *The Two Suns*, a political novel set in a sensitive period.

Why did Chiang Kuei write these two novels, which brought him so little material reward? He wrote principally out of a sense of responsibility, which a Chinese critic likened to that of the ancient Han Dynasty historian Ssu-ma Ch'ien, and which Chiang Kuei made clear enough in the introductions to both novels: to record in order to warn. Seen in this way, the novels were histories. The author was writing of real events, some of which he had seen and participated in. He was describing, as he understood them, the conditions which gave rise to Chinese Communism, so that his readers might understand. At the same time, these novels expressed his view of Communism as a Utopian doctrine which produced nihilism and unbridled selfishness in its adherents. Finally, *The Whirlwind* was a nostalgic work, recreating the rich and forever vanished environment of his childhood and youth in Hsiang-chou and Tsinan. The rituals and pleasures of Chinese New Year in an old-style great family were carefully described for readers who might never have experienced them.

The urgent impulse to record and warn was apparently satisfied in *The Whirlwind* and *The Two Suns*. His novel, *Swallow Tower*, was a detailed re-creation of Chinese society on the eve of the War of Resistance against Japan, a celebration of Chinese patriotism and endurance, but above all a psychological study of individuals and contrasting character types. Lan Wei-chen is a practical and unsentimental individual. With her positive attitude, she could fit readily into Communist society or into the bustling business world of Taiwan or Hong Kong. By contrast, the hero, Keng Tzu-hsiu, and his lover, the former prostitute Yao Liu-hua, belong to the past, and the past claims them at the end of the story.

Chiang Kuei's genius as a novelist lies in his ability to create a living world peopled with a wealth of characters in all walks of life. Such genius was well suited to deal with Republican China in its variety and misery, its presence of the old in the midst of the new. In his four serious novels—*Breaking Free, The Whirlwind, The Two Suns,* and *Swallow Tower*—he portrayed a world now gone forever, as no sociological study will ever be able to do. Through these novels, he expressed his own attitudes: a realistic appreciation of the universality of human folly and shortcomings and the advocacy of concern for the immediate as against concern for the abstract.

Notes and References

Preface

1. C.T. Hsia, *A History of Modern Chinese Fiction 1917–1957* (New Haven: Yale University Press, 1961), p. 506.

Chapter One

1. Chiang Kuei, *Hsüan-feng* (The Whirlwind) (Kaohsiung: Ch'ang-ch'eng ch'u-pan-she, 1965), p. 307.
2. Chiang Kuei, "Chi-nan liang-nien" (Two Years in Tsinan), *Tso-p'in* (Opus), 4, Nos. 3 (1963), p. 68.
3. Chiang Kuei, "Wo-ti chia-shih ho t'ung-nien" (My Family and Youth), *Tso-p'in*, 5, No. 2 (1963), p. 16.
4. Chiang Kuei, *Ch'ung-yang* (The Two Suns) (Taipei: Tso-p'in ch'u-pan-she, 1961), p. 114.

Chapter Two

1. *The Whirlwind*, p. 294.
2. Wang Yao, *Chung-kuo hsin wen-hsüeh shih-kao* (A Draft History of China's New Literature) (Shanghai: Hsin wen-i chu-pan she, 1953), p. 400.
3. *Ibid.*, p. 44.
4. *Ibid.*, p. 49.
5. *Ibid.*, p. 50.
6. *Ibid.*, pp. 158–59.
7. *Ibid.*.
8. *Ibid.*, pp. 155–56.
9. Chiang Kuei, "T'u-wei" (Breaking Free), *Chung-yang jih-pao* (Central Daily News), Taipei, Febuary 24, 1970, p. 4.
10. *Ibid.*.
11. Chiang Kuei, "Chiang Kuei *tzu-chuan*" (Chiang Kuei's Autobiography), *Hsin-hsia* (Neo-Cathay), 3 (1969), p. 101.

Chapter Three

1. Chiang Kuei, "Chiang Kuei's Autobiography," p. 103.
2. Chiang Kuei, "Liu-yüeh shuang tzu-hsü" (Preface to *Six Month Frost*), *Hsin-hsia* (Neo-Cathay), 3 (1969), p. 41.
3. Chiang Kuei, letter to C. T. Hsia, July 12, 1965.

Chapter Four

1. Wang Hsing-yen (pseudonym), *T'u-wei* (Breaking Free) (Shanghai: World Publishing Company, 1939), p. 11.
2. *Ibid.*, p. 60.
3. *Ibid.*, p. 9.
4. *Ibid.*, pp. 128−29.
5. *Ibid.*, p. 168.

Chapter Five

1. Lucy Chen, "Literary Formosa," *Formosa Today*, ed. Mark Mancall (New York: Frederick A. Praeger, 1964), p. 133.
2. Ko Hsien-ning, *Hsien-tai hsiao-shuo* (Contemporary Fiction) (Taipei: Chinese Culture Publishing Enterprise Committee, 1952), p. 224.
3. T. A. Hsia, "Taiwan," *A History of Modern Chinese Fiction 1917−1957*, p. 519.
4. Chiang Kuei, "*Chin t'ao-wu chuan tzu-hsü*" (Introduction to *Tale of the Modern Leviathan*), *Huai-hsiu-shu: Hsüan-feng p'ing-lün chi* (Sleeve Book: A Collection of Critical Articles on *The Whirlwind*), ed. Chiang Kuei (Tainan: Ch'ün-yü lou chi-yin, 1960), p. 8.
5. *The Whirlwind*, p. 5.
6. *Ibid.*, pp. 9−10.
7. *Ibid.*, p. 26.
8. *Ibid.*, pp. 36−37.
9. *Ibid.*, p. 73.
10. *Ibid.*, p. 207.
11. *Ibid.*, pp. 104−05.
12. *Ibid.*, p. 105.
13. *Ibid.*, p. 164.
14. *Ibid.*, p. 305.
15. *Ibid.*.
16. *Ibid.*, p. 375.
17. *Ibid.*, p. 376.
18. *Ibid.*, pp. 381−82.
19. *Ibid.*, pp. 505−06.
20. *Ibid.*, p. 507.

21. *Ibid..*

22. *Ibid.,* p. 508.

23. *Ibid.,* p. 519.

24. Chiang Monlin, letter to Chiang Kuei, *Sleeve Book,* p. 17.

25. Hu Shih, letter to Chiang Kuei, *The Whirlwind,* pp. i, ii, iii.

26. Kao Yang, "Kuan-yü Hsüan-feng-ti yen-chiu" (On the Analysis of *The Whirlwind*), *Sleeve Book,* p. 86.

27. *Ibid.,* p. 60.

28. C. T. Hsia, *A History of Modern Chinese Fiction 1917–1957,* p. 523.

29. *Ibid.,* p. 524.

30. *Ibid.,* p. 528.

31. *Ibid.,* p. 524.

Chapter Six

1. Chiang Kuei, *The Two Suns,* p. 5.

2. Kao Yang, "*Hsüan-feng, Chiang Kuei, Wo*" (*The Whirlwind,* Chiang Kuei, and I), *Sleeve Book,* p. 139.

3. *Ibid..*

4. *The Two Suns,* pp. 7–8.

5. *Ibid.,* p. 5.

6. *Ibid.,* p. 78.

7. *Ibid.,* p. 79.

8. *Ibid.,* p. 26.

9. *Ibid.,* p. 42.

10. *Ibid.,* p. 46

11. *Ibid.,* p. 47.

12. *Ibid.,* p. 128.

13. *Ibid.,* pp. 113–14.

14. *Ibid.,* p. 137.

15. Kuo Mo-jo, "A Poet With the Northern Expedition," *Far Eastern Quarterly,* 3, No. 4 (1944), p. 378.

16. *Breaking Free,* pp. 28–29.

17. *Ibid.,* p. 29.

18. *The Two Suns,* p. 108.

19. *Ibid.,* pp. 150–51.

20. *Ibid.,* p. 439.

21. *Ibid.,* p. 163.

22. *Ibid.,* p. 164.

23. *Ibid.,* pp. 228–29.

24. *Ibid.,* pp. 364–65.

25. *Ibid.*, pp. 340–41.
26. *Ibid.*, pp. 346–48.

Chapter Seven

1. Chiang Kuei, *Pi-hai ch'ing-t'ien yeh-yeh-hsin* (Swallow Tower)
(Kaohsiung: Ch'ang-ch'eng ch'u-pan she, 1964), p. 840.
2. *Ibid.*, p. 840.
3. *Ibid.*.
4. *Ibid.*, p. 841.
5. *Ibid.*.
6. *Ibid.*, p. 845.
7. Chiang Kuei, "Chiang Kuei's Autobiography," p. 103.
8. Chiang Kuei, "Preface to *Six Month Frost*," p. 42.
9. *Swallow Tower*, p. 843.

Selected Bibliography

PRIMARY SOURCES
Works by Chiang Kuei

1. Novels:

CHIANG KUEI. *T'u-wei* (Breaking Free). Shanghai: Shih-chieh shu-chü, 1939.
———. *Hsüan-feng* (The Whirlwind). Kaohsiung: Ch'ang-ch'eng ch'u-pan-she, 1965. Translated by T. A. Ross as *The Whirlwind.*
———. *Ch'ung-yang* (The Two Suns). Taipei: Tso-p'in ch'u-pan-she, 1961.
———. *Ch'un-ch'eng* (Spring City). Taipei: Tung-fang t'u-shu kung-ssu, 1963.
———. *Pi-hai ch'ing-t'ien yeh-yeh-hsin* (Swallow Tower). Kaohsiung: Ch'ang-ch'eng ch'u-pan-she, 1964.
———. *Chu-men feng-yü* (Turmoil among the Prosperous). Taipei: Lien-ho t'u-shu kung-ssu, 1967.
———. *Fen-ch'ing-chi* (Burnt Memory). Taipei: Lien-ho t'u-shu kung-ssu, 1967.
———. *Hsi-yen* (The Wedding Feast). Taipei: Chung-hua tien-shih ch'u-pan-she, 1972.

2. Short Fiction:

———. "Pu-ho chiao-ti hsieh-tzu" (The Shoe That Didn't Fit). *Cosmorama*, Hong Kong, n.d., pp. 26–29.
———. "Ah-yüan." *Tso-p'in* (Opus), 3 (1961), pp. 27–33.
———. "T'ao-hua wan" (Spring Freshets). *Chung-hua ch'ing-nien (Chinese Youth Quarterly)*, 4 (1971), pp. 84–94.

3. Essays:

———. *Huai-hsiu-shu: Hsüan-feng p'ing-lun chi* (Sleeve Book: A Collection of Critical Articles on *The Whirlwind*). Ed. Chiang Kuei. Tainan: Ch'un-yü lou chi-yin, 1960.

————. "Pai-fa" (White Hair). *Tso-p'in*, 3, No. 2 (1961), pp. 55—58.

————. "Wo-ti chia-shih ho t'ung-nien" (My Family and Youth). *Tso-p'in*, 4, No. 2 (1963), pp. 16—18.

————. "Chi-nan liang-nien" (Two Years in Tsinan). *Tso-p'in*, 4, No. 3 (1963), pp. 67—70.

————. "Liu-yüeh shuang tzu-hsü (Preface to *Six Month Frost*). *Hsin-hsia* (Neo-Cathay), 2 (1969), p. 40—43.

————. "Chiang Kuei *tzu-chuan*," (Chiang Kuei's Autobiography). *Hsin-hsia*, 3 (1969), pp. 101—104.

————. "Chen-ch'eng yü tzu-yu" (Sincerity and Freedom). *Hsin-hsia*, 6 (1969), pp. 83—85.

————. "T'u-wei" (Breaking Free). *Chung-yang jih-pao* (Central Daily News), Taipei, February 24, 1970, p. 4.

————. "Feng-pao lang-ya" (Stormy Shantung). *Chung-hua jih-pao* (China Daily News,) Taipei, 1972.

————. "Shang-shih yü kan-chiu" (Mortally Wounded and Thinking of the Past). *Tu-li wan-pao* (Independent Evening News), Weekly Literary Supplement, June 4, 1972.

SECONDARY SOURCES

HSIA, C. T.   *A History of Modern Chinese Fiction 1917—1957*. New Haven: Yale University Press, 1961. 2nd edition, rev., 1971. Appendix 2, pp. 555—61. This is the best criticism on Chiang Kuei. The book itself is unrivaled as an introduction to twentieth-century Chinese fiction.

HSIA, T. A.   *The Gate of Darkness: Studies on the Leftist Literary Movement in China*. Seattle: University of Washington Press, 1968. This book contains six long essays, helpful in understanding the literary and political world of Chiang Kuei's generation.

WU, LUCIAN, ed.   *New Chinese Writing*. Taipei: The Heritage Press, 1962. This collection of fiction, poetry, and casual essays by writers and poets on Taiwan contains Lucian Wu's translation of Chapter 21 of *The Whirlwind*, under the title "Snakes and Ghosts."

Index

(The works of Chiang Kuei are listed under his name)

Anhwei, 58

Borodin, Michael, 37, 42, 46, 114, 115
British, 15, 38, 41, 44
British Concession, 43, 113

Canton, 21, 36, 37, 40, 41, 42, 102, 113
Carlson, Evans F., 61
Central China Post, 44
Central Daily News, 68, 69, 99, 133, 137, 149
Central Military and Political Academy, 120
Central Party Affairs monthly, 52
Central Youth Bureau, 41,, 42
Chang Chien, 107
Chang, Eileen: *Yang-ko* (The Rice-sprout Song), 102
Chang Hsüeh-liang, 47
Chang Jen-min, 57
Chang T'ien-i, 100
Chang Tso-lin, 44
Chang Tsung-ch'ang, 39, 45, 126, 128
Chang Tzu-chung, 128, 129
Chang Tzu-p'ing, 49
Changsha, 46
Chan-kuo-tse, 24
Chao K'uang-yin, 73
Chekiang, 28, 34
Ch'en Ch'eng, 64, 65
Ch'en Ch'i-ying, 76, 77
Ch'en, Eugene, 115
Chen, Lucy, 76
Ch'en Tu-hsiu, 147
Chen Yi, 64
Chen-chiang, 53
Cheng Ch'eng-kung (Koxinga), 64, 65
Cheng Chen-to, 48
Ch'eng Fang-wu, 49
Cheng Po-chi, 49, 50
Ch'eng T'ieh-wu, 77; *Nü fei-kan* (The Girl Bandit Cadre), 77
Christianity, 99, 104-105, 116

Chiang Kai-shek, 41, 45, 46, 62, 102
Chiang Kuang-tzu, 51
Chiang Kuei: adoption, 21, 22, 23; association with Wang Hsiang-ch'ien, 27, 29, 30, 35; bankruptcy, 65, 142; caretaker, 65, 66, 67, 142; childhood, 17, 18; children, 59, 66, 142; during war, 57, 58, 59, 60, 61, 62; education, 23-25, 26, 27, 35, 55, 143; emigration, 63, 65; first love, 33, 34, 52, 53, 54; in Canton, 40, 41; in Hankow, 42, 44, 47; in Hsüchow, 55, 56; in Peking, 55; in Shanghai, 48, 52, 53, 54, 62, 63, 142; in Taiwan, 63, 64-70, 140, 142; in Tsingtao, 38, 39; names, 17, 57, 61; parents, 17, 63, 143; trial and appeals, 67, 68, 69, 131; wife Yen Hsüeh-mei, 52, 53, 58, 59, 65, 67
WORKS: ESSAYS:
"*Chen-ch' eng yü tzu-yu*" (Sincerity and Freedom), 144
"Chiang Kuei *tzu-chuan*" (Chiang Kuei's Autobiography), 143
"*Chi-nan liang-nien*" (Two Years in Tsinan), 142-43
"*Feng-pao lang-ya*" (Stormy Shantung), 143
Huai-hsiu-shu: Hsüan-feng p'ing-lün chi (Sleeve Book: A Collection of Criticism on *The Whirlwind*), 97
"*Pai-fa*" (White Hair), 142
"*Shang-shih yü kan-chiu*" (Mortally Wounded and Thinking of the Past), 143-44
Ting sheng ch'un-ch'iu (Annals of a Prosperous Age), 70, 144
"*Wo-ti chia-shih ho t'ung-nien*" (My Family and Youth), 142
WORKS: NOVELS:
Chin t'ao-wu chuan, 79, 97, 99, 103; *See also Hsüan-feng*
Chu-men feng-yü (Turmoil among the Prosperous), 133, 135-36

Ch'un-ch'eng (Spring City), 68, 69, 133-35, 149
Ch'ung-yang (The Two Suns), 39, 42, 47, 67, 70, 102-24, 142, 149, 150; publication, 67, 103
Fen ch'ing-chi (Burnt Memory), 133, 136
Hei-chih mien (The Face of Blackness), 54, 78
Hsi-tso (Exercise), 54
Hsi-yen (The Wedding Feast), 133, 137-40
Hsüan-feng (The Whirlwind), 22, 27, 32, 46, 65, 68, 70, 76-101, 102, 122, 131, 143, 149, 150; criticism, 97-101; publication, 65, 78-79; title, 79
Pai-kuan (White Coffin), 54
Pi-hai ch'ing-t'ien yeh yeh hsin (Swallow Tower), 69, 70, 125-32, 150; publication, 69, 130
T'u-wei (Breaking Free), 35, 56, 57, 60, 62, 70, 71-75, 78, 115, 132, 148, 150
WORKS: POETRY:
Only poem, 34-35
WORKS: SHORT FICTION:
"Ah-yüan," 141-42
Liu-yüeh shuang (Six Month Frost), 69, 140
"*Pu-ho chiao-ti hsieh-tzu*" (The Shoe That Didn't Fit), 140-41
"*T'ao-hua wan*" (Spring Freshets), 144
Chiang Meng-lin (Chiang Monlin), 48, 97, 98
Chiang Pai-li, 48
Ch'ien Chung-shu, 100
Ch'ien-t'ang River, 34
China Daily News, 69, 143
Chinese Left-wing Writers League, 51-52
Chinese Young Writers' Association, 97
Chinese Youth Anti-Communist National Salvation League, 97
Ch'ing Dynasty, 16, 17, 18, 20, 21, 47, 137, 143, 144
Chin-hua, 34
Chou Tso-jen, 48
Chu Cheng, 86
Chu Hsi-tsu, 48
Ch'ü Shih-ying, 48
Chu Teh, 47
Ch'uang-tsao she. See Creation Society

Chun-ch'eng, 15, 16, 17, 18, 19, 20, 21, 22, 63, 142, 143
Chungking, 57, 58, 59, 60, 61, 62, 91
Chung-kuo kuo-min-tang (Chinese Nationalist Party). *See* Kuomintang
Chung-kuo tso-lien tso-chia lien-meng. See Chinese Left-wing Writers League
Chung-kuo wen-i hsieh-hui (Chinese Literary Association), 76,
Comintern, 36, 37, 42, 46
Commercial Press of Shanghai, 48, 104
Communist Party, 32, 37, 44, 45, 46, 48, 51, 61, 62, 98, 102, 103, 122, 148
Confucius, 15, 78, 98, 116
Creation Society, 49, 50, 51

Eighth Route Army, 92

Fang Ch'i, 103
Feng Yü-hsiang, 46, 47
Fifth War Area, 57, 59, 61, 144
French, 41, 44
French Concession, 45, 104
Fu-hsing-kuan (Restoration) Central Training Institute, 59, 60
Fukien, 64

Germans, 15, 16
Goethe: *The Sorrows of Young Werther*, 26, 49
Golden Lotus, 25
Gourmont, Remy de: *A Night in the Luxembourg*, 50

Han River, 59, 128, 142
Hangchow, 34
Hankow, 18, 41, 43, 44, 107, 113, 114, 118, 119
Hankow Herald, 44, 45
Hanyang, 18, 19, 41, 114
Honan, 15, 48, 57, 58, 72, 73, 144
Hong Kong, 40, 41
Hopei, 15, 144
Hsia, C. T., 69, 76, 79, 97, 100, 101
Hsia, T. A., 77, 97
Hsia Tou-yin, 45
Hsiang-chou, 16, 17, 20, 29, 32, 33, 102, 142, 150
Hsiao-shuo yüeh-pao (Fiction Monthly), 49

Hsin wen-hsüeh (New Literature), 62
Hsin-yüeh (Crescent Moon Monthly), 51
Hsü Chih-mo, 51
Hsü K'o-hsiang, 45
Hsü Ti-shan, 48
Hsüchow, 55, 56, 70, 125, 126, 127
Hu Chien-shu, 19
Hu Shih, Dr., 27, 51, 68, 97, 98, 99
Hu Yeh-p'in, 148
Hua Kang, 39
Huang-ch'uan, 57
"Humane Literature," 49, 51
Hunan, 43, 46, 106
Hundred Flowers Period, 149
Hupei, 57, 58, 59, 61, 144

Independent Evening News, 144
International Settlement, 45

Japan, 50, 55
Japanese, 15, 16, 38, 56, 57, 58, 59, 61, 64, 92, 107, 128
Ju-lin wai-shih (The Scholars), 99

Kaifeng, 48
Kao Yang, 99, 100, 103
Kao-mi, 63
Keng Chi-chih, 48
Kiangsi, 32, 46, 98
Kiangsu, 55, 58
Kiaochow, 15
Kiukiang, 43
Ko Hsien-ning, 77
Kuan P'an-p'an, 127, 129, 130
Kuan Yü, 73
K'ung Ling-ching, 62
Kuo Mo-jo, 26, 41, 49, 114; *Shen-nü* (The Goddesses), 49
Kuo Shao-yü, 48
Kuomintang, 32, 35, 36, 37, 39, 40, 41, 42, 43, 45, 47, 48, 52, 61, 62, 73, 86, 103, 122, 123, 148
Ku-shih-yüan, 24

Lao She, 100
Lao-ho-k'ou, 57, 58, 59, 144
Lao-tzu, 98
Left Kuomintang, 38, 42, 44, 45, 46, 55, 112, 114, 122
Lei Chen, 78

Levenson, Joseph, 148
Li Ch'ing-chao, 15
Li Ta-chao, 30, 45
Li Tsung-jen, 59
Liang Shih-ch'iu, 51
Lin Shih-ts'un, 103
Literary Research Society, 48, 49, 51, 54
Liu E: *Lao Ts'an Yu-chi* (The Travels of Lao Ts'an), 15, 99
Liu Hsin-huang, 77
Liu Yü-ch'ün, 41, 42
Lo Hua-sheng, 49
Lo River, 73
Loyang, 72, 73
Lu Hsün, 51; "Diary of a Madman," 26, 84; "K'ung I-chi," 26; *Na-han* (The Outcry), 26; "The True Story of Ah Q," 26, 51
Lun-yü (Confucian Analects), 24

MacFarquhar, Roderick, 149
"Ma-jih" Incident, 45
Mao Tse-tung, 30, 43, 47, 98
Mao Tun, 48, 49, 50, 51, 54, 57, 60
Marxism, 29, 30, 31, 35, 50, 80
Marxist Research Society, 30
Maupassant, de: "The Diamond Necklace," 27
May Fourth Movement, 28, 29, 81, 103, 123, 136, 144, 147
May Thirtieth Incident, 38
Mencius, 15
Ming Dynasty, 64, 92
Mount T'ai, 15

Nanchang, 46
Nanking, 45, 46, 47, 52, 53, 58, 62, 71, 115, 128, 144
National Daily, 57
National Government, 42, 44, 61
National Peking University, 28, 30
National Revolutionary Army, 41, 42, 45, 114, 119
New Culture Movement, 29, 123, 147
New Fourth Army, 60
Nineteenth Route Army, 55-56
Northern Expedition, 39, 40, 41, 89, 103, 111, 113, 123, 137
Northern Sung Dynasty, 15

Pai-hua, 99, 147

Peking, 28, 36, 44, 47, 55, 112
Peking Translation Institute, 28
Peking University, 48
People's Liberation Army, 63
Ping Hsin, 49
Po Chü-i, 127
Propaganda Weekly, 97
Protect the Emperor Party, 120

Red and Green Gangs, 48
"Revolutionary Literature," 50
Right Kuomintang, 42
Romance of the Three Kingdoms, 15
Romanticism, 50, 51
Roy, M. N., 46
Russians, 41

Second Revolution of 1913, 36
Shakee Road, 41
Shameen Island, 40, 41
Shang Yang, 110
Shanghai, 38, 43, 44, 45, 48, 52, 54, 55, 56, 62, 63, 102, 103, 115, 125, 127
Shantung, 15, 16, 18, 19, 20, 21, 33, 48, 55, 78, 80, 86, 92, 137, 142, 143, 144
Shui-hu chuan, 15, 99
Smedley, Agnes, 48, 59, 61
Snow, Edgar, 30, 61
Soong Ch'ing-ling, 43, 46, 114
Soviet Red Army, 32
Ssu-ma Ch'ien, 150
Su Ying, 77
Sun Fu-yüan, 48
Sun Pao-ch'i, 18, 19, 20, 28
Sun Wu-k'ung, 75
Sun Yat-sen, Dr., 18, 36, 37, 43, 46, 112, 113, 143, 148
Sun-Joffe joint manifesto, 37
Szechwan, 58, 59

Tagore, Rabindranath, 27
Ta-hung Mountains, 128
Tainan, 65, 70, 102
Taipei, 70
Taiwan, 64, 134, 136, 149
T'ang Dynasty, 127
T'ang En-po, 62
Tangku Truce, 56
T'ao Ch'ien, 74
T'ao Yuan-ming, 89; *see also* T'ao Ch'ien
Teng En-ming, 30, 32

Third Front Army, 62
Three Great Policies, 37
T'ieh-lu hsüeh-yüan (Railroad Academy), 55
Ting Ling, 148; *Miss Sophie's Diary*, 147
Ting-ssu-ch'iao, 119
Tolstoy, Leo: *Resurrection*, 26, 27
Ts'ai Yuan-p'ei, 27
Tsang K'o-chia, 16
Ts'ao Hsüeh-ch'in: *Dream of the Red Chamber*, 25, 27, 99, 121
Tseng Shao-hua, 57, 58, 59, 144
Tsinan, 15, 19, 26, 30, 31, 32, 33, 52, 63, 78, 80, 102, 142, 143, 150
Tsingtao, 15, 19, 28, 35, 38, 39
Tsingtao People's Daily, 54
Tso Chuan, 24
Tu Fu, 75
T'ung Meng Hui, 17, 18, 35, 143
Tzu-yu Chung-kuo (Free China), 78

United Front, 60
United States Information Service, 79

Wang clan, 16, 143
Wang Ching-wei, 46, 115, 123
Wang Fang-tu, 16, 17
Wang Hsiang-ch'ien, 27, 28, 29, 30, 31, 32, 35, 60, 143
Wang Jen-shu, 60, 61, 148
Wang Ju-ch'i, 16, 22
Wang Lan: *Lan-yü-hei* (Blue and Black), 76, 77
Wang Lo-p'ing, 35-36
Wang Ming-k'o, 17, 22, 143
Wang Ming-shao, 17, 18, 20, 21, 35, 143
Wang Shui-chün, 30, 32
Wang T'ung-chao, 48, 49, 54, 147
Wang Yao, 50
War of Resistance against Japan, 57-62, 133, 150
Wei-hai-wei, 15
Wei Tao-ming, 64, 65
Wen-hsüeh yen-chiu hui. *See* Literary Research Society
Whampoa Military Academy, 37
White, T. H., 62
World War I, 15
Wu Ch'eng-en: *Hsi-yu-chi* (Record of a Journey to the West), 75
Wu Hsün-ch'eng, 19, 20

Wu Lu-ch'in (Lucian Wu), 79
Wu P'ei-fu, 41, 112, 113
Wuchang, 18, 41, 42, 44, 114, 120
Wuhan, 18, 41, 42, 43, 44, 45, 54, 55, 102, 107, 123

Yangtze River, 18, 43, 58, 123
Yangtze Valley, 60, 61

Yeh Shao-chün, 48, 49
Yellow River, 144, 145, 146
Yen Fu, 147
Yen Hsi-shan, 47
Yenan, 62
Yü Ta-fu, 50, 51; *Chen-lun* (Sinking), 49, 147
Yuan Shih-k'ai, 19, 36, 86, 120, 143, 147